Anybody We Know?

A COLLECTION OF MONOLOGUES

by Clay Franklin

Copyright ©, 1982, by Samuel French, Inc.

All Rights Reserved

No part of this book may be reproduced, stored in a retrieval system, or transmitted in any form, by any means, including mechanical, electronic, photocopying, recording, or otherwise, without the prior written permission of the publisher, Samuel French, Inc., 25 West 45th Street, New York, N.Y. 10036.

FORWORD

I laughed out loud when I read these monologues—usually I am a silent laugher.

I strongly recommend *Anybody We Know* just for reading—certainly for performing to a potential audience.

                                Imogene Coca

CONTENTS

LET ALICE DO IT	1
MARILYN'S CULINARY ATTEMPT	5
FATHER'S HOUR	8
A WEDDING RING FOR MAUDE	11
THESPIAN IN THE WINGS	14
AS JONATHAN REMEMBERS IT	18
THAT'S MY COUSIN	21
TOUR GUIDE	24
A WEDDING INTRUDER	27
LILY LAMARR	31
GRANDPA WAVES THE FLAG	36
A CELEBRITY IN TOWN	39
A FIVE-MINUTE WITCH	43
CELESTE AND TERPSICHORE	47
A DIVERSION FOR HAROLD	51
THE LADY PROTESTS TOO MUCH	54
A BREAKFAST REBEL	58
NORMA MEETS DORIS	61
HE PLAYS A CLEVER GAME	66
DAISY WILL TELL	69
AN AMBASSADOR OF YOUTH	73
IN MEMORY OF DAPHNE	76
HOUSEHUSBAND	80
LINGERING WITH LYDIA	84
A SUBSTITUTE FOR SANTA	88
A SCHOOLGIRL, PAST IMPERFECT	92
FAKE COWBOY	95
MELINDA MAYBELLE WHIFFLEY	99
SMALL-TIME JOE	104
YESTERDAY A STAR	110

Don't raise an eyebrow. That was Julian, my hair stylist. He has gorgeous eyelashes.

(*Glances at paper.*) End of list. And I'm exhausted. A great way to start a vacation.

(*With a sigh as she flops on chair.*) What a day. After breakfast I packed a lunch for Tommy and —

What? He's outside with his skateboard. Then I drove six screaming kids to the playground for their picnic. A dentist appointment. That was a lot of laughs. Then I came back here and mopped up the kitchen floor where the ketchup had spilled. Right at lunch time your Aunt Polly dropped in. Which reminds me — the exterminator is due next week. Then I started packing — picked up the kids — made some phone calls.

And how was your day, Perry dear? I bet you and the boys took two hours for lunch with martinis. Then you had to kiss all the pretty girls good-by. Oh, it must have been rough for you.

(*Rises.*) I forgot. I must call Peter to cut the grass while we're —

Of course I had to make a lot of phone calls. Yes, dear, I remember. After all those robberies in the neighborhood, we agreed to tell only a few people. But certain people have to know — like the milkman — the newspaper boy — the girls in my bridge club — Tommy's Boy Scout leader — We can't flap our wings like hawks and fly away.

Thank goodness for Maggie. She promised to pick

Let Alice Do It

up the mail every day — water the plants — and before dark she'll turn on a lamp. She'll even bring some of her garbage over and put it in our can out front. Why? So the house won't look deserted, dumb dumb.

Don't expect much for dinner. It'll be an omelette and a salad. And if we're lucky, a can of beer. Our refrigerator is practically naked.

(*Speaks to a boy who scoots in.*) Tommy. How often must I tell you — no skateboard in the house. Take it out in the garage. No, you can't take it along to Canada. Go on. And don't pout or you'll trip over your lip.

Perry dear, stop looking like an ad for La-Z-Boy and throw a few of your things together — since we're starting at seven in the morning. Take along your red sweater. It makes you look rugged.

(*Sits.*) Oh, of course, you must take along your camera. Praise be, you got over that stage when you took all those candid shots. The one of me in a robe and plastic curlers coming out of the bathroom — and Tommy dressed in his good suit, picking his nose — are classics. They say Canada is crawling with scenery, so click away.

(*Picks up a book from table.*) I picked up this vocabulary guide, so I can *parle francais*, a bit. It lists what to say in a restaurant, a hotel, even what to say when asking for the toilet. As you know, French is their native tongue. So I'll fracture it.

And while we're in Montreal, I must look up Helen

Werner. Remember Helen? You met her at my class reunion last summer.

Really, Perry, that's nasty. To call her "the fat dame with the nervous giggle." She's been a loyal friend through thick and thin. If you'll pardon the expression.

Why is it, dear, that you dislike most of my friends and I dislike most of yours?

(*Rises.*) But before we argue about that, let's get busy. Come on. You look for your sweater *rouge* and I'll make *une omelette*.

What? Now how did I insult your Aunt Polly? Somehow I associated her with the exterminator.(*Irritated.*) Very well. I'll say it. Like a roach, she's always around when you don't want her.(*She hurries off.*)

MARILYN'S CULINARY ATTEMPT

MARILYN, a week-old bride, has prepared her first dinner. It apparently is a failure, judging by her forlorn expression as she dials a telephone number.

Yes, Mother, this is Marilyn. I'm so miserable. . . . No, it's nothing like that. Michael is a darling. It — it's me. Something dreadful happened. Today I prepared my first dinner for the two of us — and it's a disaster.

Of course I followed the recipe. Right out of the cook book that Cousin Maggie gave me for a wedding gift. I thought it would be easy to fix a casserole — so I picked Chicken Delight. But when I took it out of the oven, it looked like Chicken Fright.

Mother, I did follow the instructions. A can of mushroom soup, rice, pieces of chicken, tomatoes, and a half cup pepper. And then the strangest thing happened. I started to sneeze. . . . Of course I shook it out of the pepper shaker and. . . . What? . . . Pepper, the vegetable? . . . Oh. But it didn't mention that in the recipe — just pepper. Well, anyhow, I put it in the oven. I just tasted it now and it's horrible. I fed it to our garbage disposal.

Yes, Mother, I'll do that. Until I take another

chance with a recipe, I'll use only frozen foods — or open a can of something. We got three can openers for wedding gifts.

What I made for dessert? Oh, Mother, don't ask. I thought a pineapple upside-down cake would be yummy. And I was so pleased how lovely it looked when I took it from the oven. I should've stopped there. But then it wouldn't be upside-down. As I turned it over the cake fell apart and dropped on the floor. The linoleum looked weird. I had to use the wet mop.

So you can see what a dismal afternoon I had. . . . Yes, Mother. Afraid I must agree with you. Before being a bride I should've spent more time over a hot stove. But somehow I never —

Oh. I must hang up now. Michael just came in. I'll call you tomorrow. Bye.(*Hangs up*)

(*She manages a radiant smile as she crosses to her spouse. A baby-talk tone.*) Hello, honey.(*A kiss.*) Of course I missed you. The day seemed so dreary without my sweetheart.

(*Sits.*) What did precious wifey do all day? Let's see. I washed the breakfast dishes. The water was so sudsy that a coffee cup fell out of my hand and broke. I know it was a wedding gift from your Aunt Minnie. But it's really her fault — for not giving us the unbreakable kind.

Just about then I got a phone call from Janet. She's getting a divorce from Ronald because they have nothing in common. She said they don't even hate the same people.

Marilyn's Culinary Attempt   7

After that I went back to the kitchen—picked up the broken pieces and cut my itsy-bitsy finger.(*Holds up finger.*) Want to kiss away the hurt? Thank you, sweetums.

Oh, of course, darling. You're starved. Yes, Michael, the dinner will be a surprise. Since—since it's been such a hot day, why don't we keep cool with a salad—that I bought at the delicatessen—with lots of crackers—ice tea—and a big scoop of ice cream for dessert.

Oh, honey, you do look disappointed. Afraid that's all I could—Well, since you ask—to be honest—all I ever cooked that turned out right—was a three-minute egg. But I'll try, darling. So please be patient.

What? You do? You love to cook? How marvelous!

All right, dear, we'll take turns fixing dinner. Do you have anything in mind for tonight? Out there in the cabinet are all those goodies we bought at the supermarket. That sounds lovely. They say you can't go wrong cooking something in a casserole. May I come along and watch?

(*Smiling as she moves away.*) Darling, let's promise that whoever does the cooking—in spite of indigestion—or if it turns out to be a disaster—we'll still be in love.

So let's have a kiss for our appetizer.(*She does so.*) Mm. We'll have more of those before our dessert.

FATHER'S HOUR

It is past the usual coming-home-for-dinner hour as ALAN PARKER returns to his residence in suburbia. He enters the living room with a weary tread.

(*Calls.*) Hi, anybody.(*He whistles a brief greeting but silence is the answer.*) It's much too quiet around here. No hi-fi blasting—no arguments going on.(*He tosses briefcase on table and then flops on chair.*)

(*Aware that someone has entered the room.*) Hi. Who's that? Debbie? Gary? Will you turn around so I know?

Oh, it's you, Debbie. Dressed in sneakers, jeans, and sweat shirt like that, I never know who's who. I should remember that Gary has longer hair.

Were you out jogging? Soccer? Oh. You're the only girl on the boys' team? And it's allowed? Oh. Congratulations, I guess.

(*Smelling an unpleasant aroma.*) Phew! Something is burning out there in the kitchen. It must be our dinner. Your mother's revenge because I'm late.

Oh. You mean Gary stirred up that smell? Well, what can you expect? As a baby, his favorite toy was an egg beater.

Father's Hour 9

Okay, Debbie. I know that look. What do you want now? What! No, I will not buy a scuba suit for your birthday—so you can play tag with a whale.

Go on. Cry all the way to the shower.(*Rises.*) What I need now is a drink.

(*He addresses another family member.*) Ah. Here is Chef Stinko himself. Gary, what did you scorch out there? You tried to bake a coconut fluff. What's that? It sounds like a shampoo. Oh, a cake. And now, the fluff is a flop, huh? Well, I suppose the garbage disposal can digest it.

How's that again? You want to enter a cake baking contest? Well, cheer up. The booby prize may be a can of air freshner. Now go out there and clean up the mess. If your mother sees that it may discourage her from fixing dinner. And I'm on my way for a drink.

(*Another member has appeared.*) Oh, hello Linda. Sorry I'm late. The traffic was unbelievable. Four lanes jammed. A traffic light not working. Sorry if you had to keep dinner waiting.

The kitchen may be a mess. Gary tried baking a cake but Betty Crocker let him down.

Care for a drink? Now what's so important that we can't have a martini first?

Okay, Linda. Have it your way. I'm sitting.(*He does so.*)

No, I don't think I forgot anything. Was I supposed to bring something from the supermarket? What's so special about today? It's Friday, April ninth.

Oh, oh. I did it again—forgot all about our anniversary. All of twenty, isn't it?

I'm sorry, hon. Look—why don't you put on your blonde wig and we'll go out for dinner somewhere? And a movie after that—if we can find one that isn't X rated.

(*Rises and crosses to mate.*) Congratulations, Linda. Here's an anniversary kiss.(*Does so.*) We survived two decades together and no scars showing. Right?

Must admit our family image is sorta kooky. Our daughter studies how to fix a clogged drain—wire an electric lamp—and plays soccer on the boys' team. While our son wears bracelets and enters a cake baking contest. I knew it was a mistake to let them wear those unisex clothes.

Here I sit dry as a stone.(*Rises.*) Oh. What shall we do about dinner?

Really? You'd rather stay here. Sure. Chicken pie and a salad will be fine. And we can open that bottle of champagne we kept for an occasion. But just the two of us, huh? Let's send the kids to the diner down the street. To celebrate we can light candles and put on those Montovani records. And for another romantic kick—we can dance cheek to cheek. So let our "Anniversary Waltz" begin.(*He goes off with a sprightly step.*)

A WEDDING RING FOR MAUDE

MAUDE LARKIN, who lives in a small town in Tennessee, is bidding good-by to the guests at her birthday party. She is middle-aged and her features are plain—in harmony with the simple dress that covers her angular figure.

It was real good of you-all to come to my party. An' thanks again for all them perty presents. Them towels an' tablecloth I sure can use. Glad ya didn't bring somethin' that I had to dust.

That's right. It all wouldn' be 'cept fer Emily here—who planned it all behind my back. It sure be one birthday party I'll never forget.

Now take care goin' home. An' Minnie, fer that cough—rub in some goose fat tonight.

Bye, Ella May. I'll see ya at the sewin' circle meetin' on Wednesday.

Clint, it was so nice of you to bring the ladies over. Drive real careful now. Bye.

(*After waving to the departing guests, she closes the door, turns and speaks to her daughter.*)

My, that was a mighty pleasant afternoon.(*Sits.*) First time I kin remember ever havin' a party jes' fer me. But then ya always remember yer ma. Even though ya live far away in the city—an' I don' see ya often—ya never forget—like Christmas an' my birthday. Havin' ya here, Emily, fer a few days is the nicest present of all.

Too bad yer pa ain' here. He would be proud of ya too. Ya always had a-hankerin' to larn an' be somebody. Even as a young un ya was smart. Ya didn' take after yer pa an' me. So now ya have a fancy job—drawin' pictures fer books an' magazines.

I remember how ya'd set at the table in the cabin, an' draw sech perty birds, butterflies, an' flowers. I kept a few of 'em all these years.

Mighty nice of ya to say that, Emily. Whatever I did fer ya I did gladly. I didn' mind sewin' fer folk—an' sell crops from the patch—jes' so ya got a good larnin'.

I declare. Look at the time. I'll fix some supper an'—

What? This ring I'm wearin'? Why, honey, that's my weddin' ring. No, I reckon ya didn' see it before 'cause—Foolish me, I lost it a long time ago. It happen, I reckon, when we moved from the cabin in the mountain an' come here. Lucky that I found it—jes' a while ago—in a box of ol' papers an' things.

Now I better go to the kitchen an' fix them taters the way ya like 'em.

(*She rises, moves away a few steps, then hesitates.*) Emily, 'tain't so—what I jes' said. I didn' lose this ring.(*Sits.*) I never had one. Never in my life did I

A Wedding Ring For Maude   13

own a ring or jewelry of any kind. Always felt I wasn' perty enough—or that we could use that money fer somethin' to wear.

I had nothin' to show that I was married—like all the other women folk I know. There they be—all wearin' a weddin' ring. Ella May an' her big mouth said, sorta makin' fun, that mebbe I never was married. That riled me. Goodness knows who else she babbled it to. I had to do somethin' to show 'em.

Then one day I looked in my Sears-Roebuck book. There was all them perty weddin' rings. So I sent fer one—the cheapest—an' never said a word about it. Now I wear it an' say that I jes' found it. I know it's wicked to say an awful lie like that. Emily, can ya understan' why I did it?

Bless ya, honey. But—but there's more I should tell ya. An' I hope ya can forgive me.

What Ella May said was true. Yer pa an' me never git married. We was livin' up in the mountain then—an' no preacher was handy—so we kep' puttin' it off. But ya was baptized. We give ya a name.

Mercy. To my dyin' day I never meant to tell ya this. But since ya saw the ring—Well, ya should know the truth.

Ya mean that, Emily? It don' change yer feeling toward me? (*She clasps hands of daughter in gratitude.*) Oh, Emily, I—I ain't got words to say how—how happy I feel.

(*Rises*) An' now let's go an' fix some supper.(*She walks away.*)

THESPIAN IN THE WINGS

PAMELLA PRESCOTT, fortyish and lively, is savoring the pleasure of being an actress in an amateur play. She and another member of the cast have just arrived at the rehearsal hall.

I'm glad we're early, Irene—so I have time to get under the skin of my character. And that's not easy—since I have only six lines to say. But as Mr. Drake says, "There're no small parts—only small actors." But who wants to be a small actor?

Of course, Irene, I'm delighted to be in the show—even though I play a stupid maid.

Oh, someone fixed coffee already. Let's go and have a cup.(*She moves away a few steps.*)

Hello, Kitty. Did you memorize your lines? Good. Yes, you do have a prominent part.

(*Confidentially to Irene.*) In more ways than one. I think Kitty is pregnant again. If not, why does she wear a caftan to all rehearsals? Well, it better not show—since she's playing a spinster.

(*Accepting coffee cup.*) Thank you, Irene.(*Sits. Takes a sip.*) Now Irene, why do you say that? You're not miscast. You're perfect as the vicious hooker. Oh,

Thespian in the Wings 15

I didn't mean it just like that. It's your acting that's so convincing. And as a bonus you get those passionate kisses from Steve Parker. Really? Well, garlic breath or not, he's gorgeous.

Look who just came in. That Wilson youngster. (*Takes a sip.*)

Hi, Tommy. Of course I know my lines.

Bright little monster. He knows everybody's lines. There he stands backstage and smirks—whenever anyone is prompted.

That reminds me. I'm not sure how I should say my first line. I enter upstage. Eleanor and Jim follow me.

By the way, did you notice how chummy those two are? They hold hands and smooch every chance they get. And Jim has been a widower just one month.

Now about my first line. I say, "You may wait in here until Mrs. Pemberton returns." I've been practising that line several ways. "You *may* wait in here—" Or "You may wait in *here*—" How should I—

Oh, look. Vanessa just made an entrance—like a leading lady of course. I suppose she got the part because of her low sexy voice. They say drinking a lot of scotch does that. Mine is strictly ginger ale.(*Takes another sip.*)

Vanessa is so lucky. She has five costume changes in the play—and they'll be stunning.

Poor me. I'm supposed to wear a frumpy housedress. To perk it up, I thought I'd add a few touches—like a chain necklace and a frilly apron. Perhaps Mr. Drake won't even notice.

I must say he's directing the play beautifully. But instead of shuffling out after my first scene, I'd like to prolong it a bit. Like stand at the doorway, look back at the visitors, give them a nasty glance, then shrug my shoulders.

Wait, Irene, I'm still on stage. Then I'll take a piece of chewing gum from my apron pocket, pop it in my mouth and exit.

There. Doesn't that improve my scene? Yes, I know. There's only one director. But I'm going to try that tonight and see what happens.

I'll take your cup along, Irene.(*She rises and put cups on table.*)

Oh, hello Eleanor and Jim. We've been missing you. Have some coffee.

(*Returns to chair.*) Irene, did you notice how they look at each other? Pure sugar. They should pour some of that in their coffee. Guess I'm jealous because Ralph and I—Well, sometimes our looks are more sour ball.

Of course he had a tantrum when I told him I was in the play. He said if I could act, so could his mashie. What a comparison. I don't even play golf.

Oh, no. This is not my first venture on the stage. In third grade I was Betty Bloom, a buttercup. And in high school I was Innocence in a pageant. And off stage I was an echo.

I must confess I always had the urge to be an actress. But along came Ralph with that gleam in his

Thespian in the Wings 17

eye. So I played the part of Motherhood twice. Now my children are grown up. So I'll allow Ralph to play golf if he'll—

Ah, here is Mr. Drake. He's so handsome. Did you notice he wears a wedding ring—but never says a word about his wife. I'm sure there's a juicy story behind that.

Oh, we're beginning.(*Rises.*) My scene is coming up soon. Oh, Irene, isn't it thrilling? Here we were a minute ago—just ordinary people. And now all of a sudden on the stage—we can make magic!(*She scurries away.*)

AS JONATHAN REMEMBERS IT

JONATHAN PRATT, still spry at the mellow age of eighty-five has been invited to speak about a course he recently completed that improved his slips of memory. He has just been introduced to the gray-haired audience assembled in the social room of a church.

(He rises to his feet, clears his throat, arranges his tie, and begins in a flustered manner.) Well, folks, I'd like to say right here from the start that this ain't my idea—to stand up here an' bend your ear. Blame it on Charlie Waddle. He coaxed me to do it—sayin' that you'd like to hear from me direct—how that memory course I took made me remember.

For the last few years my memory was somethin' awful. Like I was always lookin' for my bifocals—when they was perched on my forehead all the time—or where I put my teeth the night before. To give you two gruesome examples. Yes, indeed. I was kept busy runnin' my own lost an' found department.

Important days I'd forget—like my wife's birthday. An' it didn't help if I'd say, "Now Bertha, how do you expect me to remember, when you never look older."

As Jonathan Remembers It 19

She'd get mad anyhow. She said if I cut my finger I'd forget to bleed.

Sometimes I think her memory is worse than mine—'cause she remembers everythin'. An' that can be aggravatin'—when she reminds me that it was her an' not the garbage that I should take out.

An' I had the same trouble mixin' up people. Like I congratulated Bertha's cousin, Jennifer, on havin' a baby—when it was Bertha's niece, Anna, who had it.

Years ago, Jennifer could've married a heap of fellas—but she waited an' got more picky. He had to be a wonder man. Now all she can do is wonder where he is.

When I told my doctor that my memory was goin' bad—he had the gall to make me pay in advance.

It's an old sayin' that to remember somethin' you should tie a string around your finger. I tried it once to remind me to mail a letter. But when I looked for it, I remembered that I forgot to write it.

Well, guess I babbled enough about how I stumbled around with my memory. Now if you're doin' the same thing, then you'll want to know about this course.

It's called—uh—Now I wrote it down in case I'd forget.(*Reaches in pocket for a slip of paper.*) Here it is. It's called "Perk Up Your Memory." It's given every Tuesday evenin' at—

Oh, no. It's Monday—'cause Bertha goes to bingo every Monday. So there's nobody home that night except Flossie, our cat. An' she don't hear too well.

But where was I? Oh, yes. So if any of you folks are interested, go to—

Golly, I can't remember the name of the school. There's a candy store on one corner an' a bank on the other. An' the teacher is young an' pretty as a peach sundae. Her name is Miss Crimp—Cramp—Crump. Somethin' like that. Anyhow, you can read all about it in these circulars right here.

An' so folks, perhaps I proved to you how memory can be improved. As you heard, I don't remember everythin'. An' then again, sometimes it's a blessin' to forget.

Whenever Bertha gets annoyed if I don't remember somethin'—just to tease her, I'll say: "Just wait. One of these days I'll meet a pretty girl. An' if I chase her, I'll still remember why."(*He attempts a bow. Then he mops brow with a sigh of relief.*)

THAT'S MY COUSIN

KATHY, a teenager, and her friend, Betty, just arrived at the airport to meet Kathy's cousin, Sandra. Judging by Kathy's grim expression, she is not joyful about this meeting.

Here we are at gate 8. And the plane is scheduled to arrive on time.(*Sits.*) Wouldn't it be terrific if Sandra wasn't on it? I know I'm a meanie to say that. But I'm shook up about the whole scene—even if Sandra is my cousin.

So I'm being goofy about it. Wait till you see her. She's a tall vanilla blonde. At least she was blonde last summer when Mother and I visited them in Cleveland—on our way to Aunt Martha. Besides this gorgeous figure—she has this low sexy voice.

No, not Aunt Martha. Sandra. She has scads of dreamy clothes—enough for every minute of the day. And around boys she's a magnet. Whatever she says is smart and witty. Compared to her, I feel like a plain nothing.

Thanks, Betty, but a glamour puss I'm not. Sure, I had to tell Steve that she was coming. We're going to that beach party tomorrow and I have to take her along. And if I know Sandra, she'll make a deliberate play for Steve.

Please, Betty, tell your brother to go along as her date. Beg or clobber him if you must. Tell him I'll bake a batch of brownies if he'll go along.

Miss Brazen Face. That's what she is. In the letter she sent Mother, she practically invited herself here — and will probably stay forever.

I said something crazy to Steve when I told him about Sandra. I said she wore falsies and was pregnant. Wild, isn't it? But he'll probably flip for her anyway — even if she is middle-aged. Twenty-four. But it's happening. Guys are going all out for older women. I wonder what happens when her face sags and all those aches begin.

You're so right, Betty. The male animal can be so fickle.

What, Betty? Where? Whee. He looks dreamy with that suntan. And he wears clothes with real class. Maybe he's a celebrity and we don't know it. But whoever, I bet he's conceited and winks at himself every time he looks in the mirror.

Oh, look. There it is. A plane just came in. Now the agony begins. It's her flight.

(*Rises.*) Come on, Betty. Let's be the welcoming committee. Oh, how I wish Sandra was fat and forty.

There. People are coming down the ramp. No, that's not Sandra. That woman is too squatty.

There she is! The one in that poisonous pink outfit.

That's My Cousin 23

Oh, I hate you, Betty, for saying that. All right. So she looks like a movie star. But don't tell her that or she'll spread it around.

Yes, I'm waving. Here we go with the happy face. A kissing cousin I'm not.

Sandra! Hi. Same here. It's peachy to see you.

This is my friend, Betty. We drove over in her car. My gadabout Mother couldn't be here. A club meeting.

Shall we pick up your luggage and—Oh, really? Your plans have been changed? Sure. Let's hear.(*Sits.*)

Yes, Sandra, you did mention Larry when I saw you last summer. He works in TV, I believe. Oh. You must leave tomorrow to meet him in New York?

Oh, I'm so glad—for you, I mean. How marvelous. You want to be a model. That's just what I told Betty—that you'd be a stunning model. Didn't I, Betty?

Well, I'm sorry, Sandra, that your visit here will be a quickie. I had all sorts of fun things planned. A beach party and—

All right. Let's pick up your luggage.(*Rises and moves away.*) Oh, Sandra, I simply adore your outfit. You look just like a strawberry supreme. That's an ice-cream sundae.

TOUR GUIDE

MICHAEL PARKS, an affable young man, is a courier with a group from America who are traveling in Europe. It is one of those too-much, too-soon tours. The time is morning in Florence and Michael is greeting the passengers in the bus before departing to Rome.

(With exuberance.) Good morning, everybody. Today we bid farewell to Florence and say hello to Rome.

How's that, Mr. Flynn? So she is. Florence is around you all the time.

That's his wife, you know. Early in the morning or not, Mr. Flynn is ready with a snappy punch.

(*He turns to a passenger boarding the bus.*) Good morning, Miss Dunlap. Join us. Oh? Something confidential. Well, I have no private office, so go ahead.

I'm sorry, Miss Dunlap, but you signed up with Miss Quigley, so I cannot give you a single room. Well, that's the chance you take. When you share we can't ask, "Do you snore?"

Why don't you try this little trick tonight — you

Tour Guide 25

snore first—pretending, of course. Something interesting should happen. That's the best I can do.

Did everyone move up a seat—or back a seat?

No, Mrs. Peevy. You and Mrs. Watson move front. The people on the other side of the bus move back. Yes, dear, the front seat.

(*To driver*) Okay, Joe. I'll count the victims.

Our driver, Joe, is eager to get to Rome and do what the Romans are doing. So let's see if everyone is here.

(*Counts passengers with finger motion.*) Is someone sitting there? I just see—

Oh, there you are, Miss Finch. Did you drop your dignity? Oh, your travel book. I suppose you're writing down all the points of interest. Really? Thirty-six windows in St. Mary's Cathedral. Fascinating.

(*Continues counting.*) Twenty-eight. Two are missing. Guess who? Of course the Bronsons are late again. Well, it's their honeymoon, so—

Mrs. Peevy, what are you and Mrs. Watson arguing about? Where did we have lunch on Monday? No, dear, it wasn't Baloney. It was in Bologna. Yes, we all remember. You had indigestion afterwards.

Did we all enjoy our evening?

I agree, Mr. Martin. The food is greasy. That's a good excuse to drink a lot of wine.

Absolutely. The traffic here is wild. You have to cross the street with a wish and a prayer.

How's that, Mr. Flynn?

Did you all hear what he said? "There're only two kinds of pedestrians here — the quick and the dead."

That's right, Mrs. Watson. We'll see the Colosseum in Rome tomorrow. No, they haven't fixed it up. It's still one big ruin. No, it doesn't have a gift shop.

Perhaps you'd like to know that Rome has 7 hills, 369 fountains, and 462 churches. That'll keep you busy, Miss Finch.

Yes, Mrs. Withers? We should be in Switzerland by — Let's see. Today is Thursday. We'll be there on Tuesday. So practise how to yodel. They also have lady bell ringers, if you'd like to give it a try.

No, Mr. Flynn. They're not Avon ladies.

Something wrong, Mrs. Peevy? Why doesn't Mrs. Watson agree with you? No, Mrs. Peevy, you bought a lace tablecloth in Brussels. Remember, we stopped at Market Square with all those pigeons — and what they did to your white shoes.

That's right, Mrs. Peevy. You bought those glass beads in Venice — right after the gondola ride. Yes, it was rather smelly.

What, Joe? Good. The Bronsons are coming, rah, rah.

(*Greeting the late-comers.*) Good morning, you two. Yes, we know. You overslept. Find your loveseat and we'll be off.

Okay, Joe. Take it away. Friends, Romans, and countrymen here we come.

A WEDDING INTRUDER

KATHERINE PORTER and her husband, Vernon, have just stepped out of their car and are approaching a ramshackle house. In her brisk manner Katherine is trying to smooth the ruffled attitude of her spouse.

Now Vernon, stop complaining. I know we drove almost two hundred miles to get here. But this is Judy's wedding day. Even though she didn't invite us, I feel we should be present. After all Judy is our only child. We can be thankful that after living together for almost a year, she and Lance finally agreed to get married.

Oh, Vernon, I'm sure it's nothing like that. Judy would tell me if we're grandparents-to-be. Now we must be broadminded about all this. I'm sure we'll like Lance after we get to know him.

Oh, you don't like his name. Well, it took me a while to get used to Vernon.

This must be the house. Number 224. Yes, it could use a coat of paint — and it does look ready to fall apart. But as they say — "Be it ever so humble — ."

Did you ring the bell? Please, Vernon, wipe that

gloomy look off your face. This is a happy occasion. The bell doesn't seem to work. Come on, let's walk in.

(*After pushing open the door, she crosses a few steps and calls brightly.*) Surprise! Surprise!

Oh, there you are.(*Embraces her daughter.*) Judy dear. Happy wedding day.

Yes, your father is here too. He took off from work even though it's the busy season.

Since you didn't invite us, we decided to do it on our own. We thought it would be a pleasant surprise. But from the look on your face, I think you're in shock. Well, that's better.

(*Looks about.*) So this is your little love nest. Rather bare, isn't it? Yes, I see. There're plenty of cushions on the floor. No thanks, Judy. I'll sit on this chair and your father will sit on the other one.

(*Sits.*) I don't hope we're late. In your note you didn't mention the exact time.

Good. But Judy, for heaven's sake, take off those awful patched up jeans and—What? You—you mean the bride will wear jeans, blouse, and sneakers? In other words, a slob?

Yes, I know, dear. It's your wedding—and it's casual. But must it be so—so dreary?

And that hair-do. Did you do that accidentally or on purpose? It's a mess.

Oh. I believe this is Lance. How do you do. I see you're dressed for the occasion, too. A sweat shirt

A Wedding Intruder 29

and swimming trunks. And this is the first time I've seen a groom in bare feet.

Over there is Judy's father. Or should I say, father-in-law? Excuse him if Vernon looks a little sullen. It's his sour stomach.

And where, may I ask, will the ceremony take place? Over there?(*Rises.*) In that field? How—how different.

Oh, someone just drove up on a motorcycle. The minister. How nice. He's wearing a jump suit and carrying a guitar.

(*Returns to chair.*) Will this be a regular service—or will you play the whole thing by ear? Really. How original. You will recite your own marriage vows.(*Sits.*)

And here is the young man who will officiate, I believe. Brad? How do you do. And we'll have music, I see. Will it be some sort of wedding march? You'll sing "Bang Goes My Heart." No, I never heard of it.

Tell me, Judy, is this all of us? No attendants? No bridal party? Oh, a pity they couldn't be here. Why yes, I suppose we could take their place—if you'll tell us what to do.

Oh. We shall put these vine leaves in our hair? Very well. But I'm afraid it'll be a little difficult for your father since he's bald.

Drape them around your neck, Vernon. There. It does give you dash, Vernon.

And what is this—a loaf of bread? Don't tell me I'm to carry this. All right, dear. This is your production.

A jug of wine for your father? Oh, that'll please him no end.

Judy, I'm completely baffled. What does it all mean? Oh. Brad will read a verse from *The Rubaiyat.* Let's see. It's the one that goes—

"A book of verses under the bough

A jug of wine, a loaf of bread—and thou

Beside me singing in the wilderness."

I haven't heard that since I wore bobby socks.

Judy, won't you carry something—like a bridal bouquet? I see. Is that the best you can do—one wilted daisy? And that violet in Lance's beard is most becoming.

Oh. We're beginning. Yes, Judy, we'll walk behind you.

(*Rises.*) Come over here, Vernon. And bring the jug of wine with you.

Sh! Don't grumble, Vernon. I know it all seems unreal. And I don't like it any more than you do. But since we can't change it, we may as well join them.

There's the music. Brad is banging his heart. Come on, Vernon. Let's keep in step with that rock rhythm.(*She prances off in a lively manner.*)

LILY LAMARR

LILY LAMARR, a song stylist, has just put over a medley of songs to a dull group in a sleazy bar in New Orleans. Despite her heavy make-up, a blonde wig, and glittering gown, the bloom of youth has faded.

(To patrons. Her smile softens the rebuke.) Thank ya for the applause. That makes two of ya. I get a bigger hand when I dust the piano keys.

If you lucky people are still breathin', I'll be back with more spicy songs for ya. Perhaps ya haven't noticed—I have a large repertoire—an' this dress shows it off.

An' here's Tony, our sunny, funny man to tell ya about the next act.

(She crosses to area behind a screen that serves as a dressing room. She reaches for a Kleenex from box and dabs her forehead.) Phew! We should have a fan in this orange crate.

What, Rita? You're gonna kill 'em with your dance? I got news for ya, baby. They're dead already. Ya may as well do a flag drill. But go ahead, shake your fringe an' see what pops.

Hi, Ed. Who's out front tonight—a bunch of zombies? Well, they look freeze dried to me.

Huh? Really? The guy at table three, ya say. Mr. Jackson? My type? Uh huh. I always draw the jocks who are married an' lonely. Sure, I'll have a drinkee with him.

(*Picks up a mirror to check make-up*) You gorgeous hag. Wouldn't it be great if wigs came with heads attached.(*Puts mirror aside*) Here I go with a big hello.

(*She strolls over to a small table.*) Mr. Jackson, I believe? I got your message, so—

Hey! You're Ken Jackson—Scranton, P.A.—the boy next door!(*Throws arms around him*)

Right you are. Lillian Morris. A skinny brat with freckles—that was me.(*Sits*) But how did you know? If you saw the billing out front, I'm Lily Lamarr now. An' of all the bars on Bourbon Street, how did ya pick this one? Well, ya took a chance comin' in here. Some weirdos hang around.

Oh, here's Jimmy, to take our order.

I'll go along with that. We must have a drink to celebrate.

(*To waiter*) I'll have the usual. An' Jimmy, polish up the fancy glasses. This is a super special occasion.

Tell me, Ken, what brings ya down here to New Orleans?

You're kiddin'. A plumbers' convention—an' you're one of them?

Well, that's a switch. I remember when ya were

gonna be an archeologist an' go to far places like Greece an' Egypt.

Ya can say that again. Life is a bowl of changes all right.

Uh huh. So ya settled down in Scranton, along came a special doll, an' after that a family package. Right?

That sounds neat. Ya got it all together. A wife an' two kids in college.

Here's Jimmy with our drinks.

Thanks, Jimmy. Ya did it. Ginger ale never looked so good.

(*Lifts glass*) Here's to old friends.(*Takes a sip*) They don't come around very often.

An' now, Ken, it's your turn to put the quiz on me.

That's right. While in high school all I wanted to be was an opera singer. So I went to New York to study — an' worked at Macy's to keep me there.

Then I met Ronald — a part-time actor an' a louse, as I found out later. We had a heavy romance goin'. Ya know, all those pink lights flashin'. When he found out I was pregnant, he took off an' not a word from him since.(*Takes a sip of drink*)

I wanted to keep the kid. Larry. So I took him to nursery school an' kept on workin'. But somethin' went wrong as he was growin' up. He got into drugs — got busted — an' after that he ran away. That was two years ago. Larry is fourteen now an' still missin'.

(*With a glance toward floor show.*) There. Rita did

her last bump. Let's give her a hand.(*Applauds*) She's new in show biz an' expects to be discovered by a movie scout any night now.

Tell me, Ken, did ya come here to New Orleans for a good time — or did the wife come along? Nice of her to stay at the hotel an' let ya see the night spots.

No, I'm still single. After what happened to me, marriage is scary. So I got an act together — me an' my piano. As ya heard, the songs I sing ain't arias, but I'm a performer. I got an agent. Once in a while I appear in a classy joint — an' then it can be a rat hole like this.

There it is. That drum beat is my cue. I'm on next.

Yeah, it's been terrific seein' ya again. Give my regards to Scranton.(*Shakes hands.*) Thanks, Ken. If I'm booked up that way I'll say hello.(*Rises.*) Stick around an' I'll do a song just for you. It's an oldie you'll remember.

(*She returns to dressing room.*) Yeah, Rita, ya made 'em sizzle. Now will ya move the body so I can look me over.

Tony, will ya stop messin' around with my make-up. Ya don't need it. You're the pretty one around here.

(*She sits, picks up mirror and fusses with wig.*) Yeah, I had a cozy chat. An' was I surprised. The guy was someone I used to know — from my hometown. We were kids together. Both of us were gonna be somethin' special.(*Puts mirror aside.*)

Lily Lamarr 35

No, nothin' like that. Just good friends. Yeah, like you an' me. That's right, Tony. Ya light up my life—like a firefly.

(*Rises.*) Now go out there, baby, an' give me a build-up. Make 'em believe I'm a superstar.

Note—When performing this selection, the actress should stand at center when speaking to patrons. A screen down left and chair can be a tiny dressing room. Down right is a small table with a chair below and above it.

GRANDPA WAVES THE FLAG

JOSHUA MILLER, a hearty grandfather, saunters out on the front porch of a home in a small town. A special event will be going on today. A patriotic parade will be passing by. He speaks to his daughter, Hilda, with a German accent. She is busy cleaning indoors.

(*Looks up at the sky.*) Yah. A goodt day for a parade. Vhen da bands play so lively, I feel like a boy vit a balloon.

(*Crosses to chair and sits.*) Yah, Hilda. I read da newspaper. My name vas not in da obituary column. Vhen I see it, I vill put on my Sunday suit und lie down.(*Chuckles.*)

Come out und sit on da porch, Hilda. You can mop up later. Da dust von't run avay.

Ah, here is little Fritz. Good boy. You brought a flag along to vave. You chust have to vait. In about an hour da parade vill come.

(*He speaks to a passer-by.*) Oh, good morning, Ben. Vhere are you going? Oh? You vill ride on da fire engine—in da parade? Goodt. After dat ve play checkers. Und today I beat you.

Grandpa Waves the Flag 37

Dat's right, little Fritz. Vave da flag und march around.

(*He speaks to another passer-by.*) Oh, hello, Sarah. You're all dressed up. Going to a vedding — in da city? Too bad you vill miss da parade. A vedding you can go to anytime.

Vhat, Fritz? No, America didn't alvays have a flag. Vell, sit down vonce und I tell you.

Chust about two hundred years ago — a lady vas living in Philadelphia. Ach no, she vasn't da only lady dere. I mean, Betsy Ross her name vas. She kept busy sewing dis und dat from morning to night.

Vhat you ask? Did she stick herself vit da needle? Yah, I suppose so. If she say a svear word I don't know. Dat is not in history book.

Vell, anyhow, an uncle to her husband vas a friend to George Vashington yet. So von afternoon he bring George along to see Betsy at her home.

Ach, Fritz, don't be a *dumkopf*. Dey didn't come by taxi. Dey come by horse und carriage. So George Vashington said, "Betsy, ve vant you to make a flag for our new country."

Vell, her eyes open up big. It vas such a surprise. But she agree to do it. So Betsy stitched avay right dere in her parlor.

Ach, Fritz, how you talk. Now how could she vatch television. It vasn't yet.

(*Responds to another passer-by.*) Oh. Good morning, Mrs. Kelly. No, I didn't see little Mike running around. Yah. If I see him I'll bring him over.

Vhat, Fritz? Vhy is Mrs. Kelly's belly so big? Vell, I—I guess she eats a lot of pop corn.

Hilda, did you hear dat? Yah, it vas Mrs. Kelly. Lonely she ain't. Von on da vay und four more at home. Aye, aye, aye.

Vhat, Fritz? Yah, more about Betsy. Now vhere vas I? Ach, yes. Ven da men come back a few days later, Betsy showed dem da flag. It had red und white stripes—like your flag. But da stars—sirteen of dem—von for each colony—dey chase each odder around in a ring.

George Vashington vas so pleased dat he said, "Betsy, you have done our country a great honor. As long as dis flag vaves, you vill be remembered."

So little Fritz, vhenever you vave da flag t'ink of Betsy Ross.

Vhat? You ratter t'ink of a banana split.

Ach, du lieber. A hole in your stomach you got yet.(*Rises*) Come along, Fritz, I could eat von, too. But ve don't tell your mama. She vill t'ink it's too soon after breakfast.

Hilda. Little Fritz und I vill go around und look da new fire engine over.(*He moves away.*)

Vhat, Fritz? Yah, it's bad to tell a lie. But George Vashington I ain't.(*He shuffles off.*)

A CELEBRITY IN TOWN

To celebrate the appearance of her latest novel, MELISSA BUTTERFIELD is autographing copies at an author's tea. She has returned to her hometown for this occasion. Her appearance is sleek and sophisticated which matches her personality.

(She is seated at a table and hands an imaginary book to a member of the admiring circle.) There you are, dear. I hope I spelled your name correctly. It isn't every day that I meet a Philomena Whittenpoof.

Kay, is that the last one? Good. No, darling, I don't mind getting writer's cramp doing this. It boosts my royalties. But it numbs the rump.(*Rises.*) I'll go mingle with my dear readers.

What, Kay? A cup of tea? I'd rather have a gin and tonic. But since there's no choice, pour me a cup, please.(*She moves about.*)

Oh, hello, Norma. Of course I remember you. And hated you because you always got the part in the high school play that I wanted. So I played the maid.

What, dear? Come back for a class reunion? Heaven forbid. I detest that sort of thing. It's an excuse for everyone to say, "My God, how she aged."

39

Thank you, Norma. It's my party face. You should see it in the morning.

Marie, dear. Yes, it's fun to be back in the old hometown again for a day. Longer than that would be a drag. So it's back to New York and my typewriter. We're married to each other.

Thank you, Kay.(*Accepts cup of tea. Confidentially.*) Tell me. How much longer will his hen party go on? I'm famished. One can eat just so many lady fingers.(*Takes a sip.*)

Hi, Nancy. I've been asked that question many times—why I named the book *How Bitter the Grape*. I always advise them to read it first and decide for themselves. Oh, that's not what I had in mind.(*Turns away.*)

Kay, did you get that? Nancy didn't buy a book. But she can hardly wait until the library gets a copy. Poor author loses more royalties that way.

Hello again, Lois. I love your hair-do. Of course, darling, one must chase that gray away. Yes, Lois, like my other books, this one has plenty of *erotica amorosa*. Sex, dear, sex. You won't be disappointed. (*Takes a sip of tea.*)

Ellen, dear. So good to see you again. No, I'm still single and available. Amazing. Married twice and had five children—and you still have that divine figure.

Your score is better than mine, Ellen. So far I hatched out four. Books, I mean. Maybe you didn't

A Celebrity in Town 41

know that writing is similar to motherhood. But it is, darling. You carry around the seed of a plot for years perhaps. Then the agony and joy of putting it on paper. That's the gestation period. And finally the umbilical cord is cut when you deliver the baby between a manuscript cover. So remember, Ellen, we're not just a word machine.

Yes, Angela? Oh, you read the book already. That's true. The town in the book is very much like ours. Since you ask, a few of the characters could be people I know. Oh? You think Vivian in the book might be you. Well, she's a conniving bitch. Does that fit?(*She turns away.*)

(*Returns tea cup.*) Thanks, Kay. Did you hear? I gave Angela Lewis a nasty crack. All because years ago, while living here, I had a heavy romance going until Angela came along and smashed it. You see, authors like elephants, never forget those who jab our hide.

Look over there, Kay. A man with a camera just came in. Of course. A reporter from the newspaper. That's dandy with me. I never shy away from publicity.

How do you do, Mr. James. Yes, I'm Melissa Butterfield. Of course you may have an interview. But not here with all these screaming biddies. There's a cocktail lounge across the street. Let's go there. After one of these tea parties, I need a bracer.

Kay, we're going over to the Pink Parrot. Thanks, sweetie, for arranging all of this. I'll give you a buzz before I leave. Here's a kiss, darling.

Come along, Mr. James, before you're surrounded by clutching females.

Sorry, ladies, I must dash away from my own party. But I'm leaving on the six o'clock plane. So there's just enough time for an interview. Do forgive me.(*Moves away a few steps, then a parting thought.*) I'll probably see you all in a year or so, as I'm pregnant with another book.(*Smiling and waving, she makes a hurried exit.*)

A FIVE-MINUTE WITCH

After a day spent at school, GINGER, a teenager, and her friend, Donna are having a serious rap session. It happens in Ginger's living room.

(Paces about.) But Donna, we gotta do something desperate. Our club voted for this turnabout—that the gals ask the guys to the dance. It's one week away—and no one up for grabs.

I agree. So far we're a frost to Mark and Burt. They're so popular—being on the football team. All they say to us is "hi." So we got to thaw them out and ask them in a way they can't refuse.

(Picks up a paperback book.) And that's how this will do the trick. It's that witchcraft book I told you about. Don't knock it.*(Ruffles the pages.)* Here—in this part are spells you can put on people—like making a certain person fall in love. It even tells you what to say. And right after that it happens. Doesn't that sound fantastic?

All right. So it's weird and way out, like you say. But can't you believe in it for five minutes?

Look, Donna. I got everything set up. A candle on the table—slips of paper with the boys' names on them — and I copied the incantation. That's what you say after you light the candle.

Come on, Donna. It's now or never. And Mother is out — so we'll be spared a lot of silly questions.

Okay. I'll do mine first. And don't giggle. We must be serious about this.

(*She crosses to table.*) After I light the candle, I pick up the slip of paper with Mark's name on it and hold it in my hand.(*After doing that she kneels, closes her eyes, and chants.*)

Candle light — candle bright

As the flame burns higher

Let Mark Mason only me desire.

And so my wish is granted.

Bestaberto. Bestaberto. Bestaberto.

(*After a dramatic pause, she rises.*) There. The spell is working.

Oh, you must say that funny word — bestaberto. I don't know what it means. But according to the book, it entices the inner man so he can't help being enchanted.

Sure. By now Mark should be having all sorts of passionate vibes about me. But let him simmer while you put the spell on Burt.

Go on, Donna. Do what I did. Kneel and wipe that silly grin off your face. You can read the incantation.

There. Didn't your skin tingle while doing it? Sure thing. Already Burt is in a spin about you.

What now? We call the boys on the phone and invite them. Of course they'll accept. You must hang in

A Five-Minute Witch 45

there and have faith. Putting spells on people has been practised for centuries. So who are we to turn it off.

(*Crosses to phone.*) Here. I already wrote down the phone numbers. Let's close our eyes and say bestaberto three times for luck. Bestaberto. Bestaberto. Bestaberto. Well, here goes.(*Dials a number.*)

Hello. May I speak to Mark, please? . . . This is Ginger Porter. I'm in Mark's class in biology. . . . Really? . . . Oh, I'm sorry . . . . No, nothing special. Just give him my best wishes. Bye. (*Hangs up.*)

Whee. Now I heard everything. That was his mother. Guess what? That big baboon has the measles. Yeah. Just like a six-year old. So that's why he wasn't in school today. But who knows — perhaps he's thinking tenderly of me while scratching.

Okay, Donna. It's your turn. Make your voice sexy and call Burt. Go on. You can't back out now. And remember the dance will be held at Town Hall. And explain that it's a turnabout, so you'll call for him.

Come on, Donna. Let's give another cheer. Bestaberto. Bestaberto. Bestaberto. Now go on and dial.

Oh, good. He's there. And don't stutter.

Hey, it was all over too soon. What happened? Really? You mean Sally Bagley, that fresh piece, already asked him?

What a flop. Something went wrong. According to the book, spells have worked perfectly for centuries. Perhaps by now the date has expired. Me, too. I'm all for giving this mumbo jumbo stuff back to the witches.

So who do we lasso for the dance? By now I'm sure all the choice Romeos have been asked. Well, we can always scrape the bottom and ask Harold and Chester. They're rejects because they're too brainy.

But before we suffer through that, let's go in the kitchen and have a soda.(*She scampers off.*)

CELESTE AND TERPSICHORE

CELESTE CROCKER, fleshy and fifty in flimsy attire, is practising a belly dance routine. She consults a book before executing a step. This performance is done in the privacy of her living room.

(*Reading aloud from book.*) "Raise arms overhead, then swivel hips sensuously in a circle. Repeat this movement three times."

(*Clumsily she repeats it. Then consults book.*) "Raise arms, ripple your fingers and bend the knees with a tantalizing rhythm. Repeat three times."(*She follows instructions.*) Now I'll try it with music.

(*She crosses to record player. Then repeats the movements to the accompaniment of seductive music. While so doing, Hubert, her husband, enters. Seeing him she stops suddenly. Surprised.*) Hubert! I didn't expect you for another hour.(*She hurries to record player and turns it off.*) Why are you home so early?

Oh, you had a quick lunch. I see. A sandwich and coffee next to your computer, I suppose. You make a lovely couple.

(*Sits.*) Since you ask, yes, you did interrupt. I was

right in the middle of my lesson. No, I wasn't doing the hootchy-kootchy. That's much too vulgar.

Hubert, you better sit down while I tell you this. As you know, I believe in self expression in all sorts of ways. Last month it was finger painting. Now I'm taking a course in belly dancing.

Go on, laugh all you like. To quote from the instruction book, "It will bring out facets of my personality." And it's a fun way to get rid of this butter bun.(*She pats tummy.*) And you learn it in the privacy of your home—with no husband around to snicker.

It's done wonders for Flora Crump. You know what a timid little mouse she was. Well, she took these lessons, bought a blonde wig, and now has a romance going.

No, Hubert, I'm not "wiggling my hips to catch another man," as you so crudely put it. One of those around is plenty. This is culture. And I'm doing it for my own pleasure.

All right. Call it a middle-age fling. I prefer to call it a zing. That's such a stimulating word—zing. At least I try to keep in step with today's tempo—which is more than I can say for you.

But why must I accept you as you are—when you can express a total self. If you had attended that lecture by Waldo Worthington—about mid-life transition—you'd know what I mean.

Oh, Hubert, I don't want to hear all that nonsense

Celeste and Terpsichore 49

about taking you for better or for worse. Why can't it be for the better? You should explore new channels. Goodness knows I tried. We took a trial lesson with group therapy and you hated it. And when I took you to that demonstration on body language — you fell asleep.

I suppose we had a personality clash from the very beginning. I'm Sagittarius and you're Scorpio. But I must admit, you never interfere with any of my diversions.

Now why don't you get comfy and —

Why Hubert. What is this? A present? Oh, so it is. May twelfth. Our twenty-third wedding anniversary. Thank you, Hubert dear. You always remember all those dates. I suppose it's because you go steady with a computer.

(*Pantomimes opening a small box.*) What a lovely bracelet.(*Rewards him with a quick kiss.*) Perhaps I was a bit hasty with you, dear. With all your faults I'm still fond of you.(*Slips on bracelet.*) And this bracelet is just the thing for my belly dance. It'll look stunning when I ripple my fingers in the second movement.

(*She demonstrates dance step.*) There. Doesn't that entice you, Hubert? Well, a grunt is better than no response at all.

And now, dear, why don't you go and change around. Dinner is in the oven. And when you come back I'll do the complete dance for you — with all the trimmings. I'll wear the veil with bare midriff, and a ruby in my navel. And you, Hubert, will be the sultan. Just clap your hands twice and Fatima will appear.

Who is Fatima? Oh, Hubert, can't you fantasize for a moment? It's me. Just give me five minutes and I'll be ready.(*She hurries off.*)

A DIVERSION FOR HAROLD

HAROLD HUXLEY, a harassed accountant five days per week, is anticipating a leisurely Saturday morning. He has just finished breakfast and enters the peaceful seclusion of his den.

(Calling off.) I'll be in here, Loretta. There may be a morning game on TV.(*He crosses to imaginary set and tries various channels.*) Kid stuff all over the dial.(*Snaps it off.*)

(*He strides to easy chair, sits, and stretches with a contented sigh. Reaches for a magazine.*) Oh. Following me, Loretta?

Look dear. It's Saturday morning. I don't have to catch the 8:17 train to the office. I don't have to gulp down breakfast. I can relax with a magazine. And there you stand with a list of household chores for me to do. Go ahead, read them off, if it gives you a thrill.

Put a new washer in the kitchen faucet. Honey, I told you before. To do that I need a wrench. I looked in the tool kit and it's not there. Think I loaned it to Bill Thomas and he never returned it.

Loretta, I can't call him. Right now he's getting a

sun tan in Florida. Lucky guy. While we got snow up to our rump.

Now I know what's next. Shovel out the driveway. Right? Well, let's give the sun a chance at it. It's supposed to be out tomorrow and warmer. So think of all the energy you save not driving a car.

What's next on your funny list? Oh no. Not another mirror in the bathroom. There're so many in there now that whatever I'm doing, two other guys are doing it too. Something tells me you have a Narcissus complex.

Look, honey, how about allowing me an hour to read, huh? Is that too much to ask? But I do help around the house. Don't I pay the mortgage on it?

If you're on your way to the kitchen, sweetheart, I'll have another cup of coffee—with a smile, please.

(*A quiet moment to peruse a magazine. Then another disturbance.*) Loretta, must you run the vacuum cleaner right this minute? Just because you're mad at me is no reason to—

Hey. There's the doorbell. Since you're up, will you answer?(*He pages through the magazine.*)

Wow. What a huge box? Yeah, I see it's from Gimbels. But what's in it? Oh. Just what we need—another table to clutter up the place.

(*Rising reluctantly.*) Yes, dear, I think I am able to open it. All I have to do is loosen these staples.

Oo! Right in my finger! No blood, thank you. Certainly I can do it. I had my Wheaties for breakfast. There—it's open.

A Diversion for Harold

Hey, look at this. It's all broken. Oh, it must be assembled. Dandy. They send all the pieces and we have all the fun putting it together. Where do you want to put this tinker toy? Oh, I'm sure it'll look sensational in front of the living room sofa.

(*Sitting on floor.*) Let's see. Here are the directions with a diagram yet. And what's this round metal thing? What do you mean, a lazy Susan? Oh, the table revolves, huh? Terrific. You can get tipsy watching your drink go round and round.

Now to follow instructions.(*Reading from sheet.*) "Fit piece A into piece B." If I can find piece A we're ready to begin. No, that's piece D.

How many legs is this table supposed to have? Three? Looks like two pieces make a leg. So there should be six—

Loretta, will you stop mixing up the pieces? Hey, what's that piece for? Don't see it on the diagram. Now this metal piece is supposed to fit into piece G. Where is it? Loretta, are you standing on piece G? Maybe it's still in the box. Let's get another look at the directions.

(*After consulting sheet.*) Aha. No wonder I couldn't get this crazy thing together.(*Rises.*) According to the instructions it's so easy that a child can put it together. I'm going out and find one.(*He marches off.*)

THE LADY PROTESTS TOO MUCH

ANNABELLE FRASER is comfortably seated on the veranda of her home in Georgia. Her frilly summer finery compliments her faded beauty. A neighbor has stopped by. Annabelle speaks with a charming southern drawl.

Yes, indeedy, Polly. I simply adored travelin' when I was single an' bloomin' with good health. But then I married Philip Fraser an' my troubles began. Now when I take a trip I must be ever so cautious. I have heart palpitations, you know.

That reminds me. Did I take that pink pill before breakfast? I must ask Charlotte if she remembers. You should see my collection of pills. Such attractive colors. Charlotte teases me an' says my stomach must be decorated like a rainbow.

Yes, I must say Charlotte is a loyal daughter. Guess she remembers all those times when I was mighty good to her. The pickin's were mighty lean then, believe me. An' all because my husband deserted us.

Heavens no. She'll never marry. Chances for that are mighty slim. Charlotte is thirty-two. Oh, there were a few gentlemen friends from time to time — but

The Lady Protests Too Much 55

nothin' serious. She prefers to stay in her room an' read. An' sometimes she writes stories, too. A lot of nonsense, I imagine.

Oh, must you go? Well, Polly, it was real kind of you to stop by. I'll try to come to that church meetin'—if I feel up to it.

Of course Charlotte will come along too. I wouldn't dare go anywhere without her—should one of my attacks come on.

Ah, here is Charlotte now. Polly is just leavin'. Look at that lovely pecan pie she brought over.

Della will show you out. Bye, Polly.

(*Arranges cushion on chair.*) Charlotte, did you bring along my pills? The one I'm to take every four hours? Thank you, honey. I see you brought the mornin' mail. Anythin' special—beside the usual bills? (*Takes a pill with sip of water from glass.*)

What's the matter, Charlotte? You look so gloomy—as if you were cryin'. But honey, somethin' must be botherin' you. Now sit down an' tell me.

I declare! You got a note from Jeff Morgan. An' where is he now? Savannah. An' I suppose he's still nothin' but a greasy garage mechanic? Oh, indeed. So that's the reason he wrote—to brag about his job as an electronic engineer. Really? He's gettin' married. So that's the reason why you look so dreary. Now don' tell me you still have a fancy for him. But he's been away for goodness knows how long.

Mercy me. You say he asked you to marry him three years ago. An' why didn' you accept him?

I see. So it was all my fault — because I was ailin' poorly at the time. An' so the devoted daughter had to stay behind.

May I ask, wasn't that your duty? All those years I tried to make a livin' by sewin' clothes for folks so that you could go to college. Doin' without all those fancy things that I admire so much. It wasn't easy — scrapin' them dollars together. Who else would do it — since your father ran away with that trollop. He disappeared like a thief in the night — an' never left a penny.

Little did I dream that one day, as Uncle Oscar's only livin' relative, I would inherit this elegant house an' all his money.

But enough of that. Now run along. I want to read the mornin' paper.(*She picks up newspaper and opens it.*)

Charlotte, why are you sittin' there when I — Oh. Well, if you have somethin' else to say, wait until after lunch. Charlotte, you are provokin' me. What is this decision that's so urgent.(*Puts paper aside.*)

Charlotte! You can't be serious. Do I understand that you intend goin' away — to Atlanta? I see. An interview for a job with a magazine. How nice that they liked your stories.

So you knew about this a week ago — an' never a word to me. An' now you're willin' to desert your sick mother.

Oh. So I'm pampered, am I? An' I suppose these palpitations of mine are all my imagination.

The Lady Protests Too Much

I see. Those are sharp words. So I'm selfish an' interfered with your life.

An' what will happen if you don't get that job? My, you are confident.

An' who, may I ask, is to look after me? Della? She's a servant. An' that Mrs. Peterson snoops around.

Charlotte, where are you goin'? To start packin'? You — you're leavin' today? That's ridiculous. I won't allow it.

Very well. Since you're so determined. But let me tell you this. If you go away, I shall cut you out of my will. I swear it. Oh. Mighty independent, aren't you.

And now may I have a glass of sherry for my — (*She is aware of being alone.*) Oh.(*She remains seated for a moment, then rises and paces about in a thoughtful mood. She notices another person nearby.*)

Yes, Della. What is it? All right. Go to the market. I wrote a list of what we need.

Wait, Della. I — I'll go. It'll be a pleasant walk. The jonquils an' lilacs are in bloom.

Yes, Della. I'm going by myself. From now on I shall go my way alone.(*She leaves with a forceful stride.*)

A BREAKFAST REBEL

HERMAN GOLDBERG appears grumpy as he patters toward his place in the breakfast nook. His wife, Sadie, is already seated. He speaks with a Yiddish accent.

(*Rubbing his shoulder.*) Oi! I don't feel so good. I caught a chill in the night. After breakfast I'll put on a heating pad.

(*Sits, with a groan.*) And where is the newspaper? Sadie, I don't want to play games — no hide and seek, please.

So you want to talk. Well, what's stopping you? You've been doing it these past twenty-eight years without a hitch. What's wrong with eating and talking at the same time?

And what is this? Don't tell me it's breakfast. Where are the bagels, cream cheese, and lox? All I see is pink pills — yellow pills — yogurt — and a cup of seeds. So what am I — a canary?

Ah ha. So it's rose hips and sunflower seeds I got. And tigers milk in the glass. For this I should start my day?

Yes, Sadie, I see. You have the same. So what hap-

A Breakfast Rebel

pened? All of a sudden what are you — a health food nut?

My diet is unbalanced. Phooey! Does that make me walk like I'm dizzy?

Uh huh. I am what I eat. So I'll be a rose, a sunflower, a tiger?

Oh, sure. Proper diet will make a vigorous man out of me. So what do you expect? Tarzan?

All right, Sadie, if we need more zinc, iron, and copper, I'll go around to a scrap heap and get some — but I refuse to swallow the stuff.

Oh, we eat too many poisons. So we cut out starches, sugar, cholesterol — and then what — swallow pills instead?

Now what has Clara Schultz got to do with this? I see. Because proper diet made a new woman out of Clara — it should happen to you?

Uh huh. At home she used to sit, fat and lonely. And now she go-goes with boy friends. But enough of Clara.

Tell me, Sadie, do you plan this punishment only for breakfast — or for lunch and dinner, too? Fig juice, steamed broccoli and yeast for lunch. And what to drink? Licorice root with lemon juice and honey. It sounds nauseous. I hate to ask what's for dinner.

Well, Sadie, if this is that you put on my table from now on — then I eat out.

Maybe I should sleep out, too. Maybe like Clara

Schultz you want another string on your bow. Another man to fiddle around with.

Fiddle faddle, you say. It's happening. Look at that palsy-walsy friend of yours—Pearl Finkelstein. To Abe she was always saying, "I must find myself. I must find myself." So she went away to do it—with Frank Malone. An Irishman yet.

Sadie, this is no ifs or buts. I give you one more chance. Fix up a breakfast for a *mench*. If not, I'll go—

(*He reacts to telephone bell.*) There goes the dingaling. I'll get it.

(*He rises and crosses to telephone nearby.*) Hello. . . . Oh, hello, Nat, you old goat. . . . That's right. I almost forgot about the picnic. . . . Next Sunday, huh? . . . Oh what are we having? . . . Ah, steak—chicken—roast corn. . . . Yeah, I'm drooling already. . . . Absolutely. I'll be there. But don't count on Sadie. She's on a crazy diet and—

Sadie, will you stop screaming? But all those poisons you'll eat—like starches, sugar, cholesterol— You mean it?

Hello, Nat. Excuse the higgle-haggle. Sadie changed her mind. She'll come along. See you then. Good-by, Nat.(*Hangs up.*)

Well, Sadie, I'm glad that— What are you doing? Why all the hustle and bustle with the pan? Pancakes with syrup. Now that's my baby doll talking. And am I glad you're normal again—and not a—a vitamaniac.

NORMA MEETS DORIS

NORMA CLIFFORD, dressed in flowery summer attire, is among the guests at a charity garden party. Her features are still striking, even though her figure has become matronly plump. With a drink in hand, she chats with a friend as they stroll among the brightly decorated booths and tables for outdoor refreshment.

Before we leave, Ann, let's have a strawberry frappè. Sweets are a temptation I no longer resist, since I've given up counting calories.

Let's try and sit at a table — if any are available. Over there is one. Oh. So there is. Perhaps she won't mind if we —

Ann, what is it? Do you know her? Really? You're sure it's Doris? Well! At last we shall meet. I wondered when it would happen.

But Ann, I must meet her. After all, we have a great deal in common — Gordon. Please, Ann, introduce me. I promise I won't create a scene. Come on.

(*She crosses to garden table and speaks to the stranger with a pleasant tone.*) How do you do.

That's right, I'm Norma Clifford. As my friend Ann here met you before, I asked her to introduce us.

Very well, Ann. I'll see you there in a few minutes.

Mind if I sit down? Thank you, dear.(*Sits.*) I'm visiting Ann here in Newport. It's a coincidence that you and Gordon live here now. So here we are—first wife meets wife number two.(*Takes a sip of drink.*)

Gordon often spoke of you. Doris—so blonde and pretty—and so understanding. That shade of pink you're wearing is most becoming. You wear it with such—innocence.

I'm sure Gordon mentioned me to you. Norma—the jealous, hysterical wife. Was that how he spoke of me? Oh come, my dear, don't dodge the question. Let's tell it as it is.

But Doris—if I may be so familiar—why are you sitting here alone, when— Oh, I see. Your friend went to make a phone call. That's what I call perfect timing. Otherwise this little get-together wouldn't have happened.

How is Gordon, by the way? I haven't seen him since the settlement. Yes, his vitality is amazing. I suppose he's still chairman of the board. How lucky for us, isn't it—that Gordon is so fabulously wealthy.

Tell me, Doris, how long is it—since your marriage? Almost a year. Then everything is still kisses in the morning. How well I remember.(*Gulps down the rest of drink.*)

It was a little later on that I discovered Gordon's

philandering game. At first he called it an overnight business trip. When I suspected some hanky-panky and accused him of it, he admitted having a collection of willing bed partners. He even boasted about them—like winning so many trophies. So you see—

(*Her attention is directed to a waiter standing beside her.*) Oh. Yes, thank you. I'd like another daiquiri, please.

(*To Doris.*) Won't you have something? Good for you. I never liked the stuff either, until— Well, that's another chapter.

I suppose Gordon still has the yacht? I remember when he bought it. It was the summer of Jennifer. I was along several times on a cruise and saw that affair blossom.

Gordon was accomplished at winter sports, too—skiing and all that. And so was Mimi. A little French fashion designer that he met somewhere. (*Opens handbag and glances in mirror to check make-up.*)

Perhaps you wonder what attracted Gordon to me. I was the daughter of his boss. My father set him up—showed him ways and means of getting ahead. Gordon had everything going for him to make it. I had a career then, as a writer with a magazine.(*Closes bag*)

Later on, after our marriage, I wanted children. But Gordon preferred the image of a carefree bachelor.

(*To waiter.*) Oh, here you are. Just what I need. Thank you.

(*To Doris as she lifts glass.*) Here's to—many happy anniversaries.(*Takes several sips.*)

I don't recall exactly. When you met Gordon—were you the dancer in a Broadway show? No? I remember now. It was Karen. That affair sizzled for a season or two.

What, dear? You were a typist in Gordon's office. Well, congratulations. You made a fast promotion.

Our marriage lasted almost twelve years. I didn't want to smear him with an adultery charge, so incompatibility covered it nicely—with a generous alimony, of course. Now I have an apartment in New York and another in Palm Beach—and I travel extensively. (*Gulps down rest of drink.*)

There. Does it sound stranger than soap opera? I didn't mean to reveal so much, but somehow I felt compelled to tell you. Gordon can be charming—he has many good qualities. But it may be wise to remember that sooner or later—there'll be other bed bunnies.

How to cope with it, my dear, you'll have to find out for yourself. And as a reward, you can always ask for another mink coat.

Oo, I'm running out of time. Ann is over there waiting for me.(*Rises.*) It's been so pleasant knowing you, Doris. Thank you. Say hello to Gordon for me.(*She waves a few fingers, then moves away to join her friend.*)

Norma Meets Doris

That was it, Ann dear. The meeting of the two Mrs. Cliffords.(*After a moment to reflect; with compassion.*) She's a pretty pink little thing. There she sat — so wide-eyed and naive. But me and my big mouth — I blasted the whole sad story. How could I be so awful to her. Oh, why am I such a disgusting bitch! Come on, Ann, let's go.(*Emotionally upset, she hurries off.*)

HE PLAYS A CLEVER GAME

BRUCE BENTLEY, sophisticated and smartly groomed, and his date for the evening, Julia, return to her elegant living room after a round of social activities.

(Stifles a yawn as he enters the room.) That was a large evening. Cocktails, dinner, dance, and theatre with the same faces can become awfully chummy. It's like seeing a double feature twice. But I suppose it was all a merry whirl to you, Julia. You thrive on doing the party circuit.

(Crosses to table.) Mind if I have a nightcap before I leave? After that endurance contest I need one. Will you join me?

Julia, why the silent treatment? You've been acting odd all evening.*(Pours a small one.)* And those icy looks you gave me would cool this drink.

(Crosses to chair with drink.) Anyhow, I should be annoyed at you for introducing me to Gloria Withers—with the trombone voice. When she heard I did portraits, she fastened her claws on me and insisted that I look at her collection sometime. That'll happen when we have a blizzard in July.*(Takes a sip.)*

He Plays a Clever Game 67

(*Sits.*) All right, sweetie, let's hear it. What's your gripe? By all means start at the beginning. My behavior was rude? Explain, please.

That's correct. When I picked you up here you had to open the car door yourself. Right. When we arrived at the party you did the same thing. Really? During the evening you opened and closed the car door six times. Any bruises?

Okay, so that's one offense. Ready for number two.

True. At the cocktail party I allowed you to circulate around on your own and didn't annoy you by bringing drinks.

Yes, I noticed that. You were able to put on and take off your mink stole without my help.

There. We're up to bad manners number four.

Sweetie, I didn't have a chance to ask you for a dance before I was grabbed by some eager female. They do say I'm brilliant on the dance floor.

Now at the theatre—did I make a faux pas?

Julia, we went as a group. So did it matter who one sat next to? Right again. I was sitting between Susan and Margot. Certainly I was beaming. They're gorgeous girls.

There. Is that the end of the prosecution? Good. So will you please stop pacing about while I defend myself?

(*Rises, crosses to table and returns glass.*) May I remind you, Julia dear, of our last date. At that time you bent my ear telling me about the new freedom for today's woman. That she was equal in every way to men and should not be pampered by them. She had the physical energy to accomplish any task. Remember?

(*Paces about.*) So tonight I allowed you to be liberated all the way—and look what happens. You go into a tizzy. As for me, I had a delightful time.

Hold on, my sweet, there's more. You said certain words offended you because they were too masculine. Like a fireman should be a fireperson.

May I remind you that the word female is partly male—and there's an Adam in every madam, if you'll pardon the expression.

Aha, you're fuming. That's strong language, my pet. Hold everything. Before you start throwing things, let me out of here.

(*After hurrying toward door he turns.*) Don't expect me to ask you for our next date, sweetie. I'm a liberated man.(*He dashes off.*)

DAISY WILL TELL

DAISY SPOONER, always on the scent for a morsel of news, calls to greet a new neighbor. She carries a gift — a jar of pickles.

Good morning. You're Mrs. Brady, I believe? I'm Daisy Spooner. I live across the street. Mind if I step in for a minute?(*Without waiting for a reply, she saunters into the room.*)

As a neighbor I felt it my duty to welcome you. Here's a jar of watermelon pickle I thought you might enjoy. I put them up myself.(*Places jar on table.*) That and crabapple jelly.

I see you're busy unpacking. So don't mind me. I'll just plop down here for a minute.(*Sits.*)

Where, may I ask, did you come from? Chicago? Oh, it wouldn't appeal to me. I had a cousin living there who got lockjaw.

My, that's a gaudy painting over there. It looks like an alarm clock with spaghetti wrapped around it. Oh, it's impressionistic. Hmm, I'd call it idiotic.

Oh, you painted it? Well, I suppose one gets used to it — like a hole in the wall.

So you're an artist. Not at all like the last couple

who lived here. Mr. and Mrs. Bixby. He was a plumber. He charged me ten dollars just to open up my pipes. His wife was a saleslady in a department store. Men's underwear and pajamas. That's how she got so many boy friends.

By the way, I just happened to be at the window this morning when I saw your husband going to work.

Oh, it was a friend. I see. You're divorced. Well, it seems divorces are as popular today as—single couples living together.

Oh, dear. I didn't mean to suggest that you and—

(*Embarrassed, clears her throat.*) My, that's a pretty blouse you're wearing. If there's one color I hate it's purple. But it looks so smart on you.

Where's that screaming coming from? Now I know you have two children—because I saw them slap each other in the front yard. I see. They're playing a game in the basement. It sounds like murder.

Now I don't want to alarm you, but one can't be too careful. There're so many ways youngsters can hurt themselves by playing games. I don't suppose they'd like to play parcheesi.

Oh, what a lovely flower arrangement.(*Rises.*) I have to touch it to see if it's real.(*Touches it.*) Oh, it's artificial. Yes, it did fool me. It is pretty. But after awhile it becomes just another dust catcher.

(*Moves about.*) Since you just moved in yesterday, I don't suppose you met the other neighbors in the block. So I'll acquaint you with them.

Daisy Will Tell 71

Now next door, on this side, live the Mitchells. They're attractive and young and very pleasant to talk to. But every Saturday night they throw a party that you can hear a block away.

The Blodgetts live on the other side of you. They have four youngsters—all hellions. They break windows—mark up walls with graffiti. So I wouldn't allow my children to associate with them.

Me? Goodness no. I'm still single and untarnished. But I must admit that Oscar lives with me. Now it's not what you think. Oscar is a cat.

(*Sits*) But let's go on. Now next to the Blodgetts—in the house that needs paint—lives Mrs. Hinkle. She's a strange one who never goes out—except to bring out the garbage. Although she did borrow two eggs from me for an omelet over a month ago—and never returned them.

Then across the street—next door to me—are the Belchers and a mother-in-law. Every morning—right after I had my Ovaltine—they start an argument. What it's all about I'll never know—even when I put my ear to the wall.

In the house at the end of the row—

What? Oh. You must go and pick up groceries.(*Rises.*) Well, since your car is outside—if you'll wait a minute—I'll run over and get my shopping bag and ride along with you. I'm out of liver and prune juice.

It was so pleasant having this little chat. Now I

know you so much better. You may call me Daisy — if I may call you —

Barbara? What a coincidence. One of my best friends was named Barbara. She had a peculiar virus and played the cello. She died of it. Not from playing the cello, but —

But I mustn't dally. I'll be back in a jiffy.(*Moves away a few steps then turns.*) We can have another cozy chat in the car.(*She scampers away.*)

AN AMBASSADOR OF YOUTH

SIMON SLUSHINGTON, a disciple in the practise of staying youthful, is concluding his talk before a gathering of mellowed ladies. His speech has a British trimming.

And now, dear ladies, I shall sum up my lecture — all of which is explained in detail in my book *Be Young as Springtime.* Copies can be purchased at the table in the rear.

The book is not restricted for the fair sex only. In London it's been a smashing success with the men. Although he may be bald and bulge at the wrong places, underneath it all the old chap believes he's still a Don Juan.

To stay young at heart, we must first of all eliminate depression. Not only does the face sag and look sad but the entire body becomes limp as a noodle. Now who wants to be in that miserable mess? It's all explained in the first chapter of my book, "Who's Afraid of the Big, Bad Blues?"

Before I carry on, are there any questions? Yes, madam?

No, my dear, I don't advise watching the news on

telly before you retire. It can be very depressing. Righto. You wake up with a grouch in the morning. Now I ask. Who wants to sleep with a grouch? Even if the grouch is your husband.

Our next step to keep youthful is to count those calories or that tummy of yours will be a bulging butter bun. Ladies, when that girdle pinches it's trying to tell you something.

I know a lady in London who denies that she's fat. She calls it overstuffed. A menu for each day in the week is included in the chapter, "Sugar is a Dirty Word."

Does anyone have a question or comment? Yes, madam, if you will.

By Jove, that's intriguing. Mind if I repeat it? You say your husband gave you a birthday present but you had to diet to get into it. I dare say it was a dress. Really? Oh, I say, that's jolly good. It was a Volkswagen. Splendid. And now it's happy motoring.

Let's press on. Another way to trim the figure is by exercising. But alas, when middle age comes along we meet what I call the three B's — bulge, backache, and bridgework. And for the men an extra B — baldness. For a truly slim figure, do the exercises every day that you find in the chapter, "Bend, Stretch, and Grunt."

Do we have a comment about that?

My dear lady, I heartily agree. All those vitamins that are so good for us should be in candy, pies, and cakes — instead of in something wrinkled and bitter

An Ambassador of Youth

like spinach. So ladies, you must make a choice. Do you wish to remain a plump Patsy or be a slender Sue?

And now to cheer up any lonely hearts out there. The flame of romance does not have to burn low just because you reached a certain age. It doesn't matter if the face has wrinkles. So does a prune — and it can be enjoyable. It's amazing what happy thoughts can do for the face. So if you wish to attract and be attractive, follow the instructions in the chapter, "Love — and it Isn't Valentine Day."

Perhaps someone would like to comment about a romance in her life. Yes, madam?

Really? And why don't you believe in love at first sight? I see. How awfully amusing. To be sure, you wipe your bifocals and take a second look. Another sign of love, they say, is when it steams up your glasses.

(*Glances at watch.*) Dash it all! I must push off. My plane leaves in an hour. Thanks awfully for being so responsive. I hope all of you will not only read my book — but immerse yourself in it — so that you, too, can be young as springtime. And as the poet said, that's the time when "a man's fancy lightly turns to thoughts of love." And so, ladies, romance is in. Bingo is out. Cheerio!(*He hurries off.*)

IN MEMORY OF DAPHNE

JULIE BENSON appears disturbed as she dabs a handkerchief to her eyes. A moment later she berates her husband, Claude, who is reading a newspaper in their living room.

Oh, Claude, you are heartless. Sitting there calmly reading the newspaper when we just had a tragedy. Yesterday Daphne was so alert and playful. And this morning — her dear little body cold. Never again will we see her little tail wag.

Oh, you would make a remark like that. She barked a lot because she was sensitive.

No, indeed, Claude. She will not be thrown into a dirt hole. Daphne will be buried with dignity.

Let's not argue. I already called Mr. Witherspoon and he'll be here shortly. He's the owner of the Pleasant View Pet Cemetery. Say what you like, Daphne will have a casket, a viewing, and a brief ceremony at the grave.

I'm not out of my mind. Daphne was the only living creature I could trust. All right. So I loved her more than you. She never deceived or hurt me like some people I could mention.

In Memory of Daphne 77

If she bit you, I'm sure you deserved it. And don't call her a mutt.

Oh, there's the phone. It's probably a condolence call.

(*Rises and crosses toward phone.*) Hello. . . . Oh, Miriam. . . . Yes, I'm overcome. Did Agnes tell you? . . . In her sleep on her little bitty bed. I'm so glad she didn't suffer. My day won't be the same without her. You will come to the viewing, won't you? . . . I'll let you know. I'm sure all our neighbors want to say farewell to her. Good-by, Miriam.(*She returns hand piece.*)

Claude, what did you mumble? A pesty bitch. Who do you mean — Daphne or Miriam? They never called Daphne that. Well, if she did misbehave on their pavements it was — doing what comes naturally.

(*Paces about.*) All right. So all this insanity, as you call it, is an extravagance — and I'm paying for it. So go on your merry way to the office and —

Oh. There's the door chime. It must be Mr. Witherspoon. Since you're on your way, please let him in.

(*She sinks in chair with a grief-stricken expression.*) Good morning, Mr. Witherspoon. Yes, it is a sad occasion. Sit down, please.

Daphne is a French poodle. Almost eleven years. Her horoscope sign is Gemini.

That's right. I want the deluxe service — that is, a casket, a viewing, and a farewell at the cemetery.

Oh, you brought a picture of the casket. Yes, that

one looks lovely. You say it's made of fibre glass with lace trim. It has dignity. I'll take that one.

Heavens no. I don't want Daphne to be cold. Yes, a dusty pink comforter is just the thing. How sweet. And a white satin pillow for her head. Daphne will look adorable.

And what about flowers? What would be appropriate? How clever. Three long stemmed red roses is just the thing. Daphne loved to sniff flowers.

Now for the viewing. Perhaps a few lighted candles around the casket would be effective. Thank you. And when the service starts I'll read a poem. I'll make it up.

Yes, tomorrow afternoon would be fine for the viewing. I'll have Miriam call the neighbors. What about music? I have a recording of "Stars and Stripes Forever" that she adored. Perhaps that's too lively. I know. "My Blue Heaven." That was one of her favorites. It could be played softly in the background. Do you approve? Thank you.

The cemetery—how far away is that? Oh, how nice. We'll ride there in your black Cadillac. No. My husband won't be along. He—he's allergic to funerals.

I understand you bury all sorts of pets there. Even skunks? Oh, I wouldn't like Daphne to be next to one of those. I see. They're arranged in different sections.

Yes, indeed, Mr. Witherspoon. That would be lovely—if you'd read a verse or two from the Bible. It would make it all so theological. Whatever verse you feel is appropriate for Daphne's gentle soul will be acceptable.

And will there be a marker with her name on it? That'll be fine. I'll decide what kind of tombstone later on.

When I know how to get there, I'll visit Daphne at least once a week. Since Easter will soon be here, at that time could I place a basket of jelly beans on her grave? I'm so glad. Daphne loved them so much.

I understand. She must be groomed. In your capable hands I'm sure she'll look heavenly. So you wish to take her along now? Very well.(*Rises.*) Follow me, Mr. Witherspoon.

(*She moves away a few steps, then pauses to express a new inspiration.*) Oh. If it's all right with you, Mr. Witherspoon, I'll wear my black pants and blazer—and put black polish on my nails.(*And away she goes.*)

HOUSEHUSBAND

JACK TAYLOR and his wife, Susan, are reversing roles. He will take care of the apartment and their four-year-old son, while she ventures out in the business world. It is breakfast time. Jack, wearing apron, is busy with the menu. This is the first morning of their turnabout.

Let's see. Fruit juice, coffee, cereal, toast. All ready for the taste test.

(*Calls pleasantly.*) Susan. Breakfast is ready. You don't want to be late, dear.

Michael, stop banging on the table with your spoon. Drink your orange juice. Don't gargle it.

Hi, hon. I'm doing fine. Sit down, Susan. Here's your toast. Coffee coming up. Cereal is on the table. Oops. Whenever I pour this it dribbles on the saucer.

(*Sits.*) There. I'm ready for a cup myself.(*Sips.*) Good instant coffee. And I boiled the water all by myself.

Michael, are you ready for your cereal? There. It's in the bowl.

Now Susan, don't give it another thought. We made this decision, didn't we? The newspaper folded.

Househusband

I'm out of a job. You got an offer to go back to the advertising agency. So to stay out of hock we reverse roles.

Sure thing. I can handle it easy. Just jot down a list of what's to be done each day and I'll zip through it. Michael takes a nap in the afternoon. A dandy time for me to write that novel I never had time for.

What? Yes, Michael. I can hear the cereal pop.

Yes, dear. I'll remember to give Michael a glass of milk instead of soda. Uh huh. Just one cookie with it.

Hey, look at that kid. Sticking his ear in the bowl to hear the krispies crackle.

Stop fooling around Michael, and finish your cereal. There. You spilled it all over the table.

Susan, will you— Oh, I forgot. Cleaning up a mess is my line of duty. Blessings to paper towels.

(*He rises, crosses for towel and wipes table.*) To think that once upon a time men carried clubs and spears for the hunt. Now look at us.

Oh, is it time to go?(*Salutes.*) Yes, ma'am. I'll carry out your orders to the best of my ability. Right. Dinner will be ready by six. Sounds great. That casserole and salad are easy to fix. Everything will go along like a breeze.

Michael, kiss Mommy good-by.

Bye, hon.(*Kiss.*) Have a terrific day. Okay. Call me at noon.

No, Michael. You can't go along with Mommy. Because she's gone out in the jungle so we can survive. Never mind, sonny. It's double talk.

Now that you finished breakfast, why don't you go and finish that picture puzzle. I'll read a story to you later — after I put away these breakfast things.

No, Michael. I'm not pretending to be Mommy. I'm still Daddy. I'm wearing this apron because — well, it's sort of a uniform when doing housework. Now run along and —

And there goes the phone. No, Michael. Daddy will answer it.

(*Picking up phone.*) Hello. . . . No, this isn't the lady of the house. May I ask who's calling. . . . Oh. I see. Well, thanks all the same but I don't need pantyhose right now. . . . Who am I? The househusband, sweetheart. (*Hangs up*) Let her figure that one out.

No, Michael. No television now. You can see "Sesame Street" at four. And stop pouting.

Now let's see what's on this list. (*Reading from a slip of paper.*) "Do breakfast dishes. Make the beds. Run the vacuum cleaner."

Hey there, Michael. Simmer down. None of that cry baby stuff. Get busy with that puzzle.

Now where was I? (*Resumes reading from list.*) "Mop kitchen floor. Remind Michael to go to the bathroom. He sometimes forgets. Prepare lunch. Michael doesn't like eggs or cheese. Talk to plants as you water them." She must be kidding.

Wow. Michael, what happened? Smashed it, didn't you? Don't touch the pieces. Daddy hates to see blood.

May as well add that to the list. Glue together broken ash tray.

(*Collapses in chair as he holds up list.*) Is this for real? Do all this in one day? And prepare dinner too. Housewives, wherever you are, I salute you.

(*He rises wearily*) And now to tackle those messy breakfast dishes.

LINGERING WITH LYDIA

The beach is a tempting attraction on a sizzling summer afternoon. LYDIA FINCHLEY, a fleshy matron, is wearing sun glasses, a sleeveless dress, and carries a bulging tote bag. As she ambles along the boardwalk she gushes to her companion.

Look, Madge, at the lovely seascape. Those fleecy clouds—the waves of the ocean—the sandy beach. Doesn't all that inspire you?

Madge, did you burp? Oh, you have indigestion. Well, now that you mention it, that tuna salad you had for lunch looked suspicious to me. Take a soda mint. You always carry them with you—like that umbrella.

Please, Madge, let's not have a tiff. We all know you and the umbrella go everywhere—like Mary and her little lamb.

Over there's a bench. Let's hurry over before someone— Sorry, Madge. I didn't mean to push you. Of course I didn't do it on purpose. Sometimes you're as sensitive as a bowl of jello.

(*Sits on bench.*) Here we are. Sit down, dear, and watch the bikinis go by. Every summer I promise

Lingering with Lydia 85

myself that I'll wear my bathing suit. But when I look at those playgirls prancing about—well—I'm afraid my body has gone out of style.

I tried every kind of diet—but I can't break the habit of nibbling between meals. Why are sweets and junk food so tempting? I must try carrot sticks for a change.

You're so lucky, Madge. You can eat anything and nothing spreads on you.

Really, Madge, you're so picky today. I didn't say you were skinny. Twiggy, perhaps, but not skinny.

Now let's soak up some of this glorious sunshine. So glad I brought along my suntan lotion.(*She rummages in bag and brings out various articles.*) Let's see. It's somewhere in this grab bag.

(*Lifting a book.*) Here's that obscene book I told you about that I'm reading. Filthy words on every page. Shocking. I can hardly put it down.

(*Holds up an inch of knitting.*) This is early sweater. It's to be a Christmas gift for Cousin Mildred's baby. Her fifth. Strange, she never had children when she lived in Warm Springs. But ever since she moved to Alaska she's been breeding.

(*Shows a candy box.*) My traveling companion. Nothing like chocolate butter creams to sweeten a trip.(*Takes a chocolate and munches it*) Too bad chocolate gives you a skin rash. But then I can't face a glass of buttermilk like you can.

(*Reveals an envelope.*) Oh! Here's a letter I

should've mailed last week. It's a sympathy note to Esther Wimple. She's mourning the loss of Dolores—her pet poodle. Remind me to drop it on the way back.

(*Holds up bottle.*) Here it is. It's called Satin Seduction. A pity there's no guarantee with it.

Here, Madge. Dab some on your face and see what happens. Very well. Suit yourself. But don't blame me if you turn lobster pink.

(*Rubbing lotion on face.*) Yes, Madge. I have the bus tickets in my purse. Uh huh. We'll try and get the front seat on the way back. We must be kind to your squeamish stomach.

(*Lotion is applied on arms.*) Now relax, Madge and enjoy all this sunshine for a change. You're indoors so much. Even in your apartment you only see the sun from your kitchen window above the sink.

(*Takes tissues from bag and wipes hands.*) I haven't been sunning much either—what with all the rain we had. That gave me time to do the things I loathe—like clean closets—wash curtains—

(*With a contented sigh.*) There. I'm ready to be barbecued.

Whee. Madge, look over there. Miss Strip Tease. Those huge sun glasses cover more of her than the bikini. I suppose that's her playmate—the man doing flip-ups. Really, he's Apollo come to life. What a provocative pair. I'm sure they deserve each other.

That reminds me. Did you know that Louise Badger and her new boy friend went to Cape Cod last

Lingering with Lydia   87

week? Well, the romance is all over. Why, she didn't say. Perhaps she liked him better when he wore a wallet instead of swim trunks.

But we're prattling too much. To get the full benefit of the sun's vibrations we should close our eyes and meditate.(*She does so*) Let's pretend that we're soaring—like a sea gull—and—

(*Opens her eyes.*) Madge, why are you slapping yourself? Just because a mosquito bit you is no reason to—

What was that? It sounded like thunder. Oh my! Look at those black clouds.(*She hurriedly puts articles in bag.*) I suppose it'll pour any minute. How disgusting. We pick out one day to go to the shore and we get a cloudburst.

(*Rises.*) Here it comes! Hurry, Madge, open your umbrella. You're a darling to bring it. Come on. Let's make a dash for the pier.(*She dashes off.*)

A SUBSTITUTE FOR SANTA

Having had a delectable dinner, FRED HOPKINS purrs contentedly as he enters the living room. It is a welcome retreat from the pre-Christmas madness in the department store where he is employed. His wife, Edith, follows.

Honey, that Swiss steak was superb in any language. And my favorite pie for dessert. All those special goodies and it isn't my birthday.

(*Sighs as he sits in a comfortable chair.*) Ah. Edith, do me a favor. Don't ask me to budge from this chair. Just three more mad shopping days—then no more Christmas delirium until another year. And like usual, today was no joy to the world in kiddie heaven.

Oh, sure. I got a promotion. That carnation I have to wear blinks like a beacon. They all rush to me with their complaints, exchanges, and "Where's the ladies' room?"

Mrs. Butterball wants to exchange Kermit the frog for Eloise the elephant. Or Mrs. Blabbermouth gripes because her teddy bear doesn't wink. An eye fell out. And kids—they crawl out of the woodwork and try

A Substitute for Santa 89

everything until it breaks. So do you blame me when I say *toys* is a dirty four-letter word.

No, thanks, Edith, not now. I'll have a beer later on.

Today we got a new item—Glamour Gertie. She is blonde, sexy, and is complete with cocktail dress, swim suit with matching platform shoes, a hairbrush, comb, and toothbrush.

Edith, you won't believe this. She flirts, cries, and burps—and when she wets her diaper she gets a diaper rash. All of this and Gertie too for $19.95. And some dumb kid will think Santa brought that. Poor guy. He gets blamed for all those goofy gifts.

Then goody, goody. I have another treat to look forward to—the day after—when more presents are exchanged than on Christmas.

Okay, dear. Enough shop talk. Come tomorrow it'll be there waiting for me.

I see we got a lot more greetings.(*He picks up a card from table.*) Mm, from the Ace Exterminating Company. I didn't know they cared. They'll love us when we get termites.

(*Picks up another.*) Oh, here's one with a family photo. Who are they? Marvin and Veronica Johnson. Wow, how they changed. Where're they living now? Milwaukee. I suppose those long winter nights are the reason for those six kids. Veronica is well padded—at all the wrong places. And Marvin—the part in his hair has departed. Ah yes. Hair today and gone tomorrow.

(*Reaches for another one.*) Oh. From your Aunt Sophie. I should've guessed. She always sends a card with a lot of angels. Yeah, I see she wrote a note. I bet it's the same organ recital about her gall bladder and squeamish stomach.

Honey, since you're up, would you mind bringing my slippers? And a beer would taste great.

Sure, it's almost seven o'clock. What has that to do with —

Oh? A Christmas festival for orphans at church tonight. Huh? Really? Too bad Stanley Frisby slipped on the ice. They always pick him to play Santa. Did he break anything? Sure, a sprained back can be painful.

Edith, what has all this to do with getting my slippers and a can of beer?

She did? So Stella brought over the Santa Claus suit. And what does that mean?

Oh, no! Absolutely not! No way! I shall not be Stanley's understudy. Because I haven't the blubber that he has. No, Edith, to stuff a pillow around my navel isn't the same thing. And that beard — it tickles and smothers you at the same time.

How about asking Pete Watson? He'd be perfect. He has the beard and a belly that shakes like jelly.

But why me? Here I am enjoying a relaxing evening at home and all of a sudden it's Saint Nicholas time.

Go ahead, Edith. Call me an old Scrooge who disappoints all those orphans.

(*Resigned to his fate, he speaks without enthusiasm.*) Okay, Edith, I'm hating myself. I'll do it. Where's the funny suit?

(*He rises reluctantly.*) Oh, sure. It'll give me the Christmas spirit. I'll ho ho ho all over the place.

So tell me, what am I to do? Sure. I'll bounce them on my knee before they kick me in the shins. And I hand each kid a gift. What if they want a refund?

(*As he moves away.*) I hope they don't believe all that nonsense about Santa riding in a sleigh with eight reindeer. And they better not ask me to name them. If they do, I'll tell them I came by jet.

A SCHOOLGIRL, PAST IMPERFECT

BARBARA BAKER, with hair, dress, and make-up carefully arranged for an evening out, enters her living room. She tosses her evening bag on a small table, then tugs at her girdle as she surveys the plump figure in a mirror.

(Annoyed, as she pats her tummy.) You can't win. I think thin — stretch my spine — and look at me. A bloated butter ball.

(She glances at watch, then calls toward bedroom) Charlie. It's almost six. Are you ready? *(She gives hair a few pats as her husband enters.)*

Mm, you look dashing, dear. That suit still fits nicely. It isn't fair that you can stay so thin. That tie — it's awfully loud. Really? A Christmas present from me? Well then, it'll do. And you forgot to comb your hair so that bald spot won't show.

(She crosses to window.) It's so nice of Arthur and Lucy to pick us up. *(Looks off.)* They should be here any minute. He'll toot the horn.

And please don't poke fun about Arthur's hairpiece. It's done wonders for his ego. He even wears it to bed, Lucy said.

A Schoolgirl, Post Imperfect 93

(*Sits.*) Really, Charlie, must you look so somber? We're going to have a fun evening — I keep telling myself. As I remember, you had a ball at our last class reunion. All those dances you had with Peggy Blair — your old flame.

All right, we were ten years younger. We can still swing and sway in the same old way. And if it'll cheer you up, Peggy may be there — but not with Alan. The way I heard it, she didn't marry Alan for his money — but is divorcing him for it.

Don't be silly. I was never jealous of her. At the time I was stepping out with Harvey Whitman. Remember Harvey? He was on the football team. A figure like Adonis — but a midget mind.

I never made it as an honor student, like you did. I sang off key in the glee club — and as a maid in a play, I accidentally dropped the tea things on Chester Brown's lap. He still glares at me whenever he sees me.

Charlie, can you believe it — we graduated from Maplewood High thirty years ago. Remember how we danced the jitterbug? I wore bobby socks and had a crush on Cary Grant.

Uh huh. Your pin-up girl was Betty Grable. She had gorgeous legs.

Yes, dear, we had pimples then. Now we have wrinkles.

(*She rises, crosses to table and picks up a book.*) Foolish me. I dug up our class book this afternoon.

Our pictures are in here—all smiles and innocence.(*Drops book.*) It upset me so much that I fixed myself a chocolate sundae—and loved every spoonful.

(*Moves away.*) Well, there's one consolation. Everyone at the reunion will be in the same age bracket. We're all fighting the battle of middle age—and some lost.

Okay, have your little joke. We're the Ben Gay set.

Yes, I suppose we'll stick on name cards. That way we don't have to say, "Guess who."

(*Crosses to window.*) There. I believe they're here.(*Looks off.*) Yes, they are.

(*Hurries to table for evening bag.*) Now remember, no cracks about Arthur's hair-do. And please, Charlie, smile once in a while.

(*Crosses toward door.*) Look at me. My new girdle is pinching me—yet here I go—smiling—cha cha cha.(*She does a dance step as she goes off.*)

FAKE COWBOY

SPARK DALLAS, a familiar personality on TV screens, is relaxing on the patio of his home in the San Fernando Valley. He is resplendid in cowboy regalia. His privacy is invaded by the appearance of his housekeeper.

Yeah, Bessie? Say it again, honey, an' slower. Kitty Blossom from *TV Secrets?(Rises.)* Oh, hell, I forgot all about that. She's here for an interview. I'd rather have a cactus stick me. Yeah, show her in.

(*He crosses to a portable bar and mixes a fizzy drink. Then he greets the newcomer.*) Howdy, Miss Blossom. No, ma'am, I never had the pleasure before. An' with a name as pretty as you, it should be Peach Blossom.

What'll ya have to drink? Ya won't like what I'm havin'—a bromo seltzer. It was a rough day out on location. We wrapped up *Rainbow Over the Valley.* So 'scuse me for wearin' my workin' duds.

Sure, go ahead an' mix your own. All my pals do that. An' most of 'em have their own special drink—marriage on the rocks. I had one of them too—but got a divorce an' now I never touch the stuff.(*Puts down empty glass*)

(*Strolls toward a lounge chair.*) I see ya brought a tape recorder along. So I can't dodge the quiz.(*Sits.*) Most of them magazines print a lot of hogwash about us TV folks. What I'll tell ya is straight shootin' stuff. Okay, pardner?

For those who read your magazine this should be a shocker. Today my saddle-ass rode down that sunset trail for the last time. After eleven years of doin' one series after another, I'm splittin' from all this.

That means no more contracts—no more pinnin' medals on Boy Scouts—no more autographed pictures with Smoky, my horse. I've had it up to here with this phony business an' the phony friends ya meet. But most of all I'm tired as hell of bein' phony me.

That's right, ma'am. Everythin' about me is fake. Take my name—Spark Dallas. Now who would give a kid a label like that but a studio press agent. They wanted a name with some zing to it. My real name is Howard Hinkle. Now that don't sound rootin'-tootin', does it? An' for the camera I had to be prettied up. My hair had to be tinted—an' caps put on my teeth.

Go ahead, Miss Blossom, shoot a question.

I was born in Bayonne, New Jersey—an' the only horse I ever rode was on the merry-go-round. Then I was actin' in a play off Broadway when one of them talent scouts saw me.

Fake Cowboy 97

(*Rises and paces about.*) So before ya can say hi-yi-yippee, I was out here — an' had to learn real quick how to saddle up, handle a gun, an' talk like a genuine cowboy.

All of a sudden I was another guy — on camera — off camera. I was Spark Dallas, an' I couldn't shake him off. Even when I put on my socks in the mornin', it was Spark Dallas doin' it.

It became real scary. So I went to a shrink. Analysis is the polite word for it. What I got is a split personality, he said. Half of me resents bein' this fake cowboy. An' as ya hear, I can't throw off talkin' like a buckaroo.

As ya know, cowboys are fadin' out on TV. Now it's cops an' science fiction. So it's a good time to turn in my heated swimming pool an' go back east. There's a gal there who still remembers me as Howard Hinkle. I'll do some travelin' around — without a horse — an' find some business that I —

(*His speech is interrupted by the return of the housekeeper.*) Yeah, Bessie? Al Fleming? I'll take it out here.

'Scuse me, Miss Blossom. My agent is callin'. Perhaps ya'd like to see the flower garden. It's over there.

(*Picks up telephone from bar.*) Hi, Al. . . . Congratulations for what? . . . The Bronco Bill Award. What the hell is that? . . . Al, are you sober? . . . Me? The Cowboy of the Year? . . . Look, pal, if this is a crappy joke. . . . Wow! Ya say I'll be on TV from coast to coast? . . . When? . . . Okay. I'll accept. . . . Sure, come on over. (*Stunned, as he hangs up.*)

(*He takes a few steps as if to leave, then remembers the visitor.*) Oh, damn. (*Beckons to her.*) Ya can come back now.

Look, Miss Blossom, I gotta ask a favor. Ya must erase that tape ya took. For the time bein' my plans are changed. As I heard it, I'm gettin' some sort of award. Now ain't that somethin' else? My agent is comin' over to explain.

(*Takes her arm as he leads her off.*) So can ya come back tomorrow, honey, at the same time — an' I'll spill the whole story. That's right. Spark Dallas will be around for awhile. An' I'll try to keep my split personality from showin'. (*He goes off.*)

MELINDA MAYBELLE WHIFFLEY

MELINDA MAYBELLE WHIFFLEY bursts into her luxurious penthouse living room. Her elegant gown is an original and her silver hair is dressed in an elaborate hairdo. Although her effervescent personality comes on strong, her open manner creates a pleasant impression. She is followed by Miss Scattergood, her secretary, who is carrying a sheaf of papers. Melinda greets three men who have assembled in the room.

(Effusively, with a wide gesture.) Darlings! It's so marvelous that you gentlemen could be here. I'm glad you helped yourselves to drinks and hors d'oeuvres. By now the three of you know that you have something in common. You were all married to me.
(She joins them to shake hands and give each a kiss.) Virgil. How are you? Ah, that twinkle in your eye is more devilish than ever, now that you're bald. Still the college professor, I suppose? How lovely.
(She moves away and repeats the business.) Spencer, my handsome tycoon. Stocks are doing very well, aren't they? I bless you every month when I receive my dividend check.

(*Greeting another.*) And Reginald. Or I should say, Doctor Peckham. I suppose people are still paying extravagant fees to recline on your couch.

There. Now do sit down and be comfortable. Have another drink.

No, thank you, Spencer. I'm not indulging this week.

(*Sits gracefully.*) This is Miss Scattergood, my secretary. She'll be taking notes from time to time.

I suppose you're all agog to know the purpose of this meeting. As you know, I've been married four times. I've been everywhere — done everything — twice. So Lowell Frisby, a publisher friend of mine, insists that I write my autobiography. He wants to call the book *Melinda the Madcap* because I've done so many daffy things. So of course, all of you are included.

And now we should pause for a moment and pay tribute to Alberto. As you may remember, he was my first venture into matrimony. Alas, he is now among the dear departed.

Alberto was an opera singer, if you remember. A tenor. He heard how Caruso by holding a high note could break a crystal glass. Well, Alberto wanted a bigger challenge, so he tried it in front of Macy's store window. But instead of the window bursting, Alberto did. But he is with us tonight — in that urn on the stereo cabinet.

And now Miss Scattergood will give each of you a folder. In it are facts about each of you that I recall. Do feel free to correct and add whatever you wish.

Melinda Maybelle Whiffley   101

Oh, thank you, Reginald.(*Pats hair tenderly.*) It's a new rinse. Silver Siren. They advertise it so rashly. It practically promises instant seduction. Nothing that drastic has happened yet.

(*Referring to a paper.*) While they're perusing that, Miss Scattergood, jot down a few notes. On this page I listed various amours that were sprinkled here and there. I use only their first names, so we can take liberties in writing about them.

(*Reads name from paper.*) Vincent. Ah, yes. He was a ballet dancer that I met on a cruise to Nassau. We shared a bottle of champagne together and had a gay time. Oh, dear. One has to use that word so discreetly now. Anyhow, he wrote delightful love poems—to boys. In the book we'll stretch Vincent to a few paragraphs.

(*Reads another name.*) Ricardo. He was a matador I met in Madrid. Poor darling, he fooled around with the bull too long. A tragedy. To pay my respects, for a day or two I had ripe black olives in my martinis.

After Ricardo we'll leave a lot of space to mention those other mad Madrid nights.

(*Glances at paper.*) Omar. Just to mention his name and I see the hot white sands of Egypt—and all those horrible flies. We met somewhere between the pyramids and exchanged a passionate kiss. After that I had dysentery for two days.

(*Another name from paper.*) Pierre. He had magnetic eyes and a charming accent. He operated a health retreat in Monte Carlo. I went there and was massaged with a peacock feather. It was positively sensational. We'll go into more detail about that.

Oh, here is Virgil. Sit down, dear.(*Glances at his report.*) Now let's see. Did you bring your activities up to date? My, I'm overwhelmed. All those degrees—all that intellect. That's really what caused our divorce. I always saw you as a mental giant. I tried to read the classics. I adored the limp leather binding. But I never could get past that first chapter. Thank you, Virgil dear. You'll be the man of letters in my book. Now go back and finish your drink.

There you are, Miss Scattergood. We'll use a few of those Latin phrases Virgil wrote down. It'll appeal to our upperbrow readers.

And here is Spencer. Please sit down, my dear.(*Glances at his report.*) Oh, I'm sure *The Wall Street Journal* would love this. It's amazing, Spencer, how you can predict the rise and fall of the stock market. And yet it was a gypsy fortune teller who predicted our divorce. This will do nicely, thank you, darling.

Oh, you must run along? Of course. Don't be late for dinner. I understand perfectly. I was a suspicious wife myself on several occasions.(*Offers her hand.*) Many thanks, Spencer dear, for joining the survivors. Let's keep in touch. Good-by, darling.

And now Reginald, if you're ready.(*Looking at his report*) Oh my, I'm impressed. You have clients from London and Paris. Should I ever believe that I'm a pink rabbit I'll make an appointment.

Yes, Miss Scattergood?(*Glances at watch.*) So it is. (*Puts aside papers*) Forgive me, darlings, but I must dash. I'm seeing a hockey game with Gregory. And for that I must slip into something nonchalant. Gregory is a rugged, outdoor type. His muscular control is amazing.

(*Rises.*) So have more drinks and stay as long as you like. Miss Scattergood will remain and take any additional notes. And when the book is out you'll get autographed copies.

(*Shaking hands.*) Seeing all of you again did bring back memories. The fun we had together—and the bickering—the laughter and the tears. It was like a rerun of an old Barbara Stanwyck movie. Farewell, darlings.(*She throws two kisses and hurries off.*)

SMALL-TIME JOE

It is show time 1933 in the corroding splendor of the Orpheum Theatre on Main Street. The Saturday matinee includes news, a feature movie, and on the stage—live—four acts of vaudeville. The quality of these range from mediocre to fairly good.

JOE BARLOW, dressed in undershirt and trousers, is seated behind a make-up table in a dingy dressing room. He speaks to his wife, Mabel, who is repairing a costume.

(Peering in a mirror, about to apply hobo make-up.) Cheer up, Mabel. Just three more shows to go. Then ya can unlax the girdle for two weeks. So flash those spangles, honey.

(He reaches for a tissue and dabs his forehead.) Yeah, ya can fry a herring in this cracker box. But come tomorrow ya can sit by the fan in our apartment. An' for a change we got time to unpack our trunks—until we play the parks in June. An' for next fall, Roy has promised a bigger an' better tour.

(Turns toward wife; enthused.) Zowie! With new costumes an' a different flashy finish that I got in mind, we'll knock 'em bowlegged. Then Palace

Small-Time Joe

Theatre here we come. I don't care if our act follows Fink's Mules, we're gonna play there — or my name is Joe Klutz.

Aw, Mabel, don't give me that all the time. Sure we got a depression. There're bread lines an' guys sellin' apples on street corners. But President Roosevelt's new deal will click an' conditions will perk up. Vaudeville will become bigger than ever.

Naw, these talkin' pictures won't last. There's nothin' can take the place of real, live flesh up there — to talk, sing, an' dance. According to *Variety*, Sophie Tucker is packin' 'em in at the Palace right now.

Say, is Rose in her dressin' room? Did ya notice, here of late she don't leave the hotel when we do. An' she don't hang around with us as much, either. Is a romance cookin' that I don't know about?

Well, I ain't so sure. A few times this week I caught her backstage bein' chummy with that Swedish acrobat an' his muscles.

I know, I know. Rose ain't a child. Sure, she needs some of that lovey-dovey stuff now an' then. But nothin' steady except Mickey Mouse — 'cause her career comes first. The kid has so much talent that it lights up a stage. Another Marilyn Miller — that's what she can be.

Now why do ya say that? Rose loves show biz — almost as much as me. So why —

(*A knock on the door interrupts his speech.*) Yeah? Come in. We're decent.

(*He addresses a blonde, dimpled beauty.*) Hi, Rosie, baby doll. Good. Ya're all ready to go on. Did ya have lunch? There's a sandwich an' some coffee over there.

Oh. Yeah, I see. The flower came off your dress. Take over, Mabel. Ya shake a mean needle.

(*A circle of rouge is placed on the tip of his nose.*) Aw, quit gripin', you two. Sure, we played some rat holes this season. But all that will be different come September. After we perk it up with jazzy costumes—an' add another dance number for you, Rosie—our act will be a smasheroo.

Hey, Rosie, why the droopy face? Which reminds me, ya've been actin' sorta strange all week. So if somethin' is botherin' ya—

Don't interrupt, Mabel. We got time. The movie is still on. The gangster ain't bumped off yet.

Come on, baby doll, sit down an' spill it. Go ahead.

(*He stares at her, disbelieving what he heard.*) Hold the phone. Did I hear it right? Ya—ya got to quit the act? What's that supposed to be—a belly laugh?

Hey, slow the patter. Ya're goin' to Youngstown tomorrow—to meet—your husband? For real?

Mabel, did ya hear? How can ya sit there an' not raise an eyebrow. Oh, ya knew. It was a secret between you girls.

(*Stunned.*) Jeez! What am I supposed to ask now? Who's the guy? When did it happen? Why was I left out in the cold?

Small-Time Joe 107

Frank Walsh, huh? Yeah, I remember. He came backstage once or twice when we played Ohio—an' he works in a bank. They ain't doin' so good right now.

Uh huh. Ya met him in Atlantic City last summer. An' when did ya ring weddin' bells?

Hear that, Mabel? It happened in March—before a matinee—when we played Elyria.

(*Dejected, his hands drop heavily on his lap.*) Jeez. Ya had a weddin'—an' we ain't invited.

No excuses. An' ain't I got a right to raise one helluva stink?

It's been The Three Barlows since ya were twelve. An' with all that practisin' ya're now a great dancer. Ya give our act class. With the right breaks ya could be a headliner in a year or so.

Now ya want to toss all that away. For what? So ya can cook breakfast for two—wash out shirts an' socks—

Aw, come on. Ya've been hearin' too many love songs. Well, ya do say it with real heart.

So what can I say? Guess I gotta grin' an' accept it, baby.

(*His arms reach out to embrace the weeping daughter.*) Hey, those tears will smear your make-up. All good wishes, Rose. An' may none of your kids be acrobats.

Say, ya better scram. It's almost time for the overture.

(*After a pause*) Jeez, Mabel, I can't believe it. Today is the last time we'll ever do our act together—the three of us. Without Rose we'll never play the Palace.

(*To break the mood, he combs his hair with a rapid motion.*) Now what kind of a gag is that? It's not a good time to quit.

Okay, so Rose bows out. We can do a double—like we did before. We'll add some new jokes. Ya can do that Spanish dance again with castanets.

(*He reaches for a shaggy orange wig and arranges it over his hair.*) An' me—instead of doin' pratfalls an' juggle dishes for laughs—I could be a smoothie— wear a top hat an' tails. We may not make the Keith circuit but—

What's eatin' ya, Mabel? Ya say that every year at the end of the tour 'cause ya're tired. Sure, sometimes the room at the hotel has only runnin' water an' roaches—we go to eateries that hand ya greasy spoons—an' sit up overnight until the train gets to our next town. That's all part of the razzle-dazzle of bein' a trouper.

So ya really mean it this time? Ya want to bow out. Well, remind me to ask ya again next week.

(*He hurries behind the screen to put on his costume. Most of him is concealed except his bright-topped head.*) Now I know you're daffy when ya say that. Me quit—when all this is my life's blood? Did ya forget that at age three I performed with my parents in the circus? It's been show time ever since—carnival, burlycue, an' vaudeville. An' here I wanna stay—even if ya walk out on me.

Small-Time Joe 109

A snappy song an' dance man—that was me when we met—an I could do it again. A dye job would cover the gray around the ears.

(*He emerges fully dressed in his loose fitting hobo suit.*) I'd rehearse some new songs—an' then go into my soft shoe routine.

(*A quick examination in the mirror*) If I do toot my own horn, I'm in dandy shape for forty-five.

(*He plunks on a tattered hat at a sporty angle. Then he struts toward the door.*) Come on, honeybunch. Let's go out there an' knock 'em dead.(*He does a brisk exit.*)

YESTERDAY A STAR

LOLA MARLOWE, a movie actress of former glory, sweeps into the outer office of Lou Shapiro, a Hollywood producer. Her face and figure are a bit more fleshy than the stunning beauty of the fifties. Lola is also remembered for her tempestuous personality. Appearing very superior in her elegant finery, she speaks to a receptionist.

(With authority.) Good morning. Mr. Shapiro is expecting me. I'm Lola Marlowe. Please announce me.

No, dear, not Lola Marlene. Lola Marlowe. I'm afraid the name means nothing to you.

No, thank you. I don't care to sit down.(*Glances at watch*) It's exactly eleven o'clock. The time for my appointment. And I don't want to be kept waiting.

(*Paces about.*) Really? You do recognize me. Perhaps you remember one of my— You mean I was on a TV commercial—cleaning a bathroom bowl? How repulsive. My dear, I've never been that desperate to stoop so low.

Yes? I can go in now? Thank you.

(*She strides toward center into the private office.*

Affable.) How do you do, Mr. Shapiro. No, you never had the pleasure of meeting me before.(*Sits in a regal attitude.*) At the studio I was associated with only established producers. While you, of course, are so new in the business.

That's why I was surprised to read in the *Reporter* that you will do a remake of *Bitter Destiny*. I created the role of Nina Blake. It was one of my biggest triumphs. Did you see it? I'm glad you did.

A good performance? I was magnificent. All of my fans agreed that I should've won the Oscar that year. Joan, Bette, and Barbara were dying to play the part. Yes, we were the golden girls of the fifties.

At that time you were in New York — pushing carts of clothing along Seventh Avenue. You see, I do know something about your background.

So when Bob Baker, my agent, called to tell me that you wanted me to appear in *Bitter Destiny* again, I was delighted.

Now I can play Nina with more depth. It will have a more modern appeal — an older woman who attracts a younger man. Don't you see? I kept a copy of the scenario. Changes must be made in the dialogue, of course. But gutter talk is out. And —

Please don't interrupt. I always had the privilege to choose my leading man. So if he's available, I'd like Keith Linden to play —

Mr. Shapiro, I think it's rude of you to —

What! You — you have the gall to sit there and tell

me the part of Nina will be played by someone else? Who would dare to play it?

(*With venom.*) Carol Ashley! She can't act her way out of a plastic bag. Not a glimmer of star quality. They say she can't even ad lib a belch. If she plays Nina Blake it will be a travesty.

(*Rises and paces.*) So—if I'm not to play Nina—may I ask why the hell you sent for me?

Yes, I recall the part of Pauline—the faded burlesque broad. She has two good scenes. Now don't tell me you want to offer that part to me?

You bastard! You know what you can do with it. I see. It would be a great publicity stunt, wouldn't it? Lola Marlowe plays a bit role in a remake of film she starred in twenty-two years ago.

(*She towers above him*) Hear this, Mr. Shapiro. I'm not that desperate to make a comeback. Scripts are still being sent to me. They're full of violence and nudity, so I turn them down. I still get heaps of fan mail. And thanks to a generous alimony, I live comfortably in Beverly Hills.

That's right. I'm a has-been. But I have the satisfaction of being a real pro. I had training in the theatre. I played all sorts of parts before I faced a camera.

As for you, Mr. Shapiro, you're nothing but a promoter—with a calculator where your heart should be. And that's my exit line.(*She departs in the manner of a movie queen.*)

(*In the outer office she almost collides with a woman.*) Oh. Excuse me. I didn't see—

(*With tone of honey.*) Yes, my dear, I'm Lola Marlowe. Thank you for remembering. Yes, there's a possibility I'll be doing another picture soon. I have several to choose from. I agree. As a producer, Mr. Shapiro is one of a kind.

(*Hissing to herself as she strides off.*) A stinking son-of-a-bitch!

Other Books by CLAY FRANKLIN

These Mortals Among Us
You're the Show
It's My Turn
Boy Appeal
Mixed Company
I Step From a Famous Story
Two For a Happening
Skits for the Young at Heart
Ten Plays of Terror